T0081026

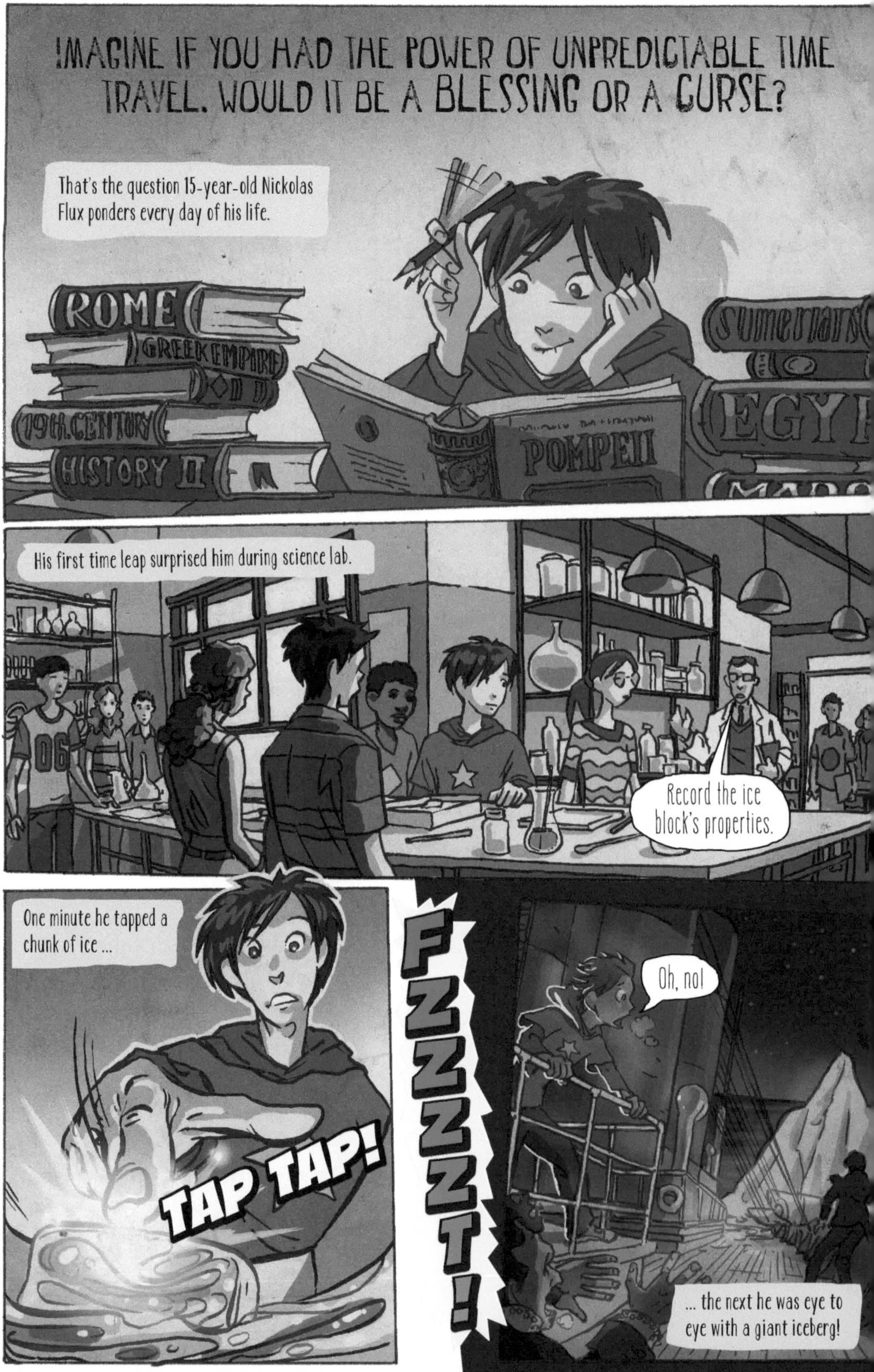
IMAGINE IF YOU HAD THE POWER OF UNPREDICTABLE TIME TRAVEL. WOULD IT BE A BLESSING OR A CURSE?
That's the question 15-year-old Nickolas Flux ponders every day of his life.
ROME
GREEK EMPIRE
19th CENTURY
HISTORY II
POMPEII
His first time leap surprised him during science lab.
06
Record the ice block's properties.
One minute he tapped a chunk of ice ...
TAP TAP!
FZZZZT!
Oh, no!
... the next he was eye to eye with a giant iceberg!

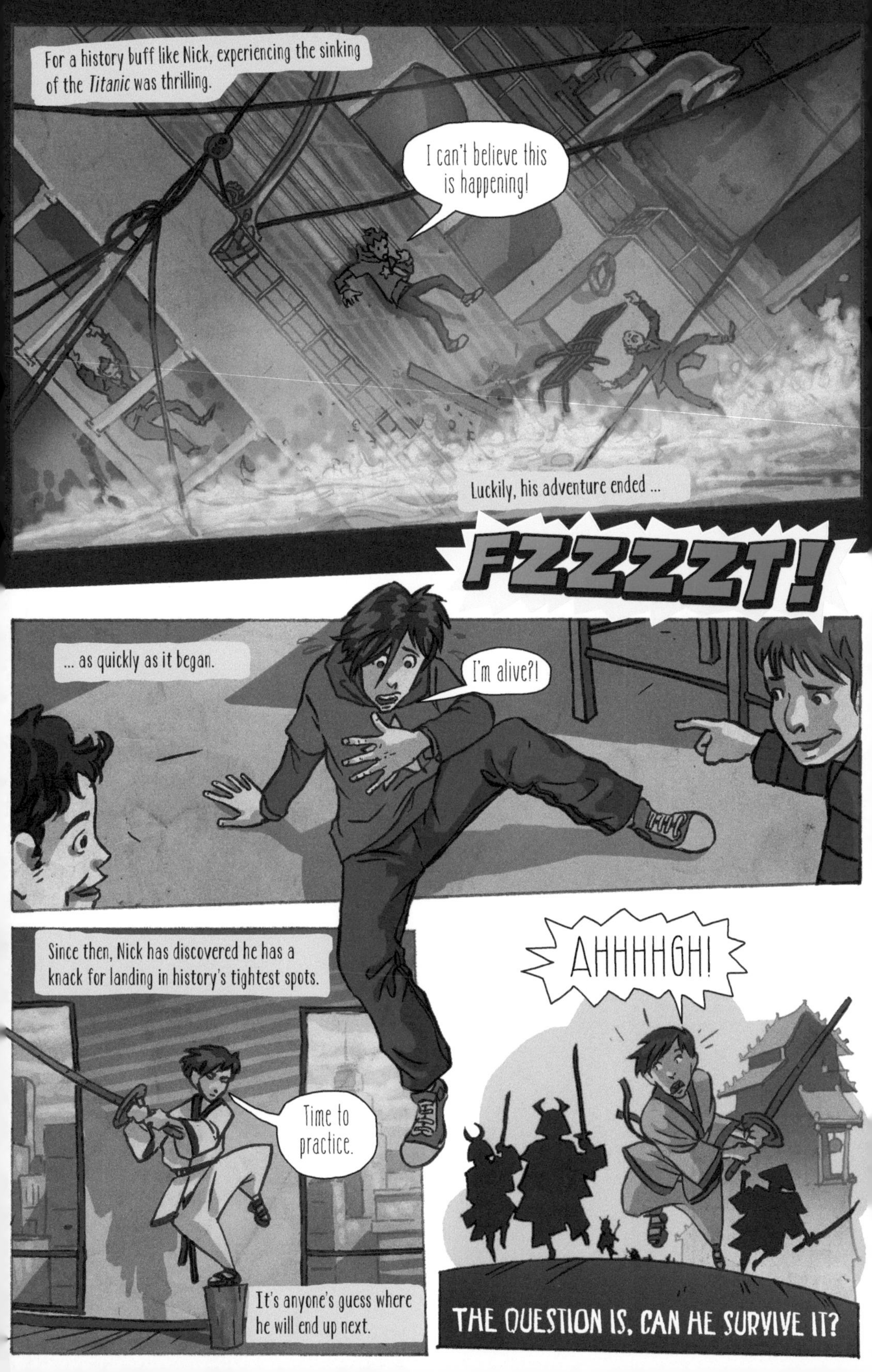
For a history buff like Nick, experiencing the sinking of the *Titanic* was thrilling.
I can't believe this is happening!
Luckily, his adventure ended ...
FZZZZT!
... as quickly as it began.
I'm alive?!
Since then, Nick has discovered he has a knack for landing in history's tightest spots.
Time to practice.
It's anyone's guess where he will end up next.
AHHHHGH!
THE QUESTION IS, CAN HE SURVIVE IT?

Nickolas Flux HISTORY CHRONICLES

TRACKING AN ASSASSIN!

NICKOLAS FLUX and the Assassination of Abraham Lincoln

BY Nel Yomtov
ILLUSTRATED BY
Amerigo Pinelli

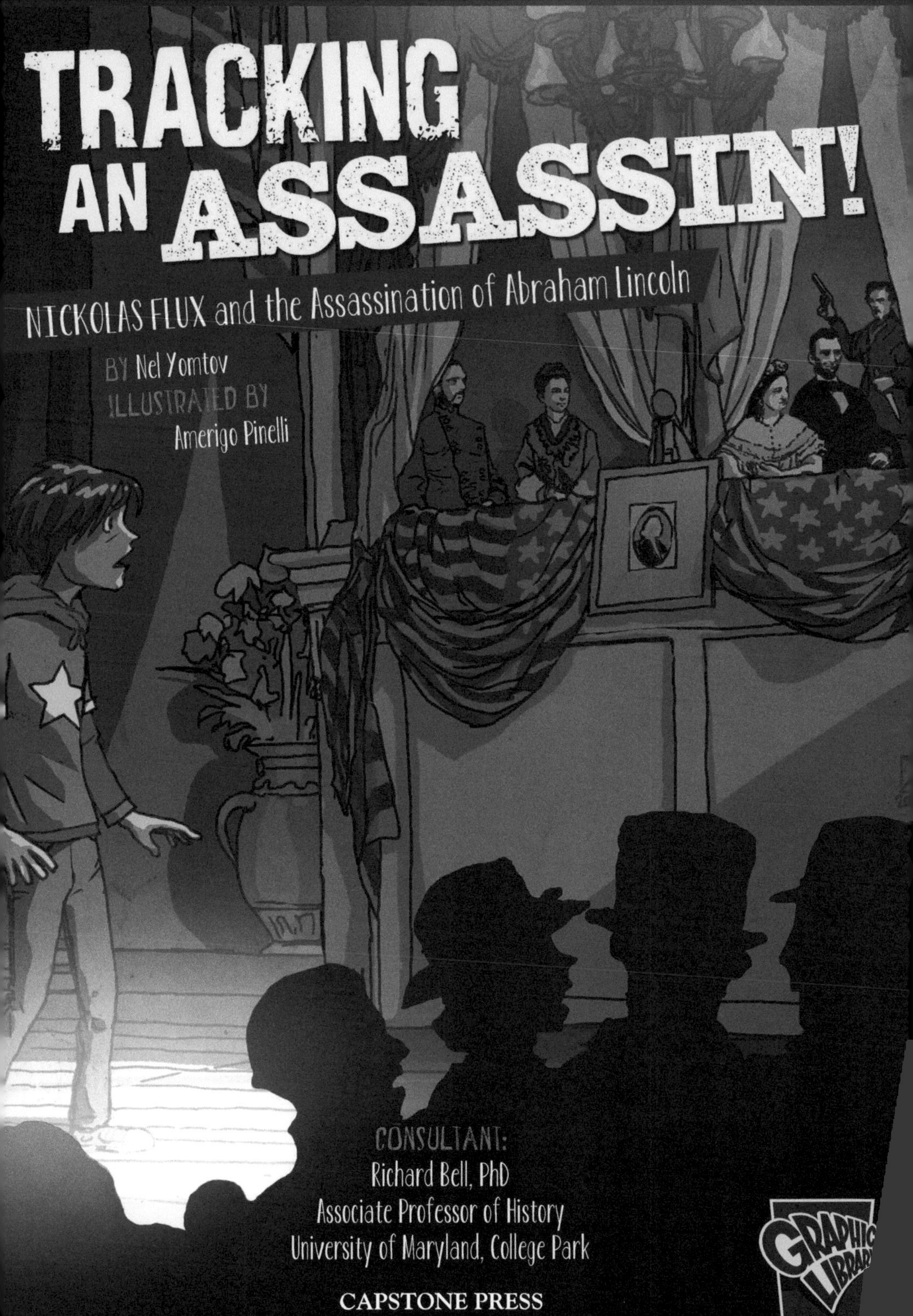

CONSULTANT:
Richard Bell, PhD
Associate Professor of History
University of Maryland, College Park

CAPSTONE PRESS
a capstone imprint

Graphic Library is published by Capstone Press,
1710 Roe Crest Drive, North Mankato, Minnesota 56003
www.capstonepub.com

Library of Congress Cataloging-in-Publication Data
Yomtov, Nelson.
Tracking an assassin! : Nickolas Flux and the assassination of Abraham Lincoln / by Nel Yomtov ; illustrated by Amerigo Pinelli.
pages cm.—(Graphic library. Nicholas Flux history chronicles)
Includes bibliographical references and index.
Summary: "In graphic novel format, follows the adventures of Nickolas Flux as he travels back in time to the assassination of Abraham Lincoln and joins the hunt for John Wilkes Booth"—Provided by publisher.
ISBN 978-1-4914-0252-8 (library binding)
ISBN 978-1-4914-0257-3 (paperback)
ISBN 978-1-4914-0261-0 (e-Book PDF)
1. Lincoln, Abraham, 1809-1865—Assassination—Juvenile literature. 2. Lincoln, Abraham, 1809-1865—Assassination—Comic books, strips, etc. 3. Booth, John Wilkes, 1838–1865—Juvenile literature. 4. Booth, John Wilkes, 1838–1865—Comic books, strips, etc. 5. Assassins—United States—Biography—Juvenile literature. 6. Assassins—United States—Biography—Comic books, strips, etc. 7. Graphic novels. I. Pinelli, Amerigo, illustrator. II. Title.
E457.5.Y66 2015
364.152'4092—dc23 2014003731

Photo Credits:
Design Elements: Shutterstock (backgrounds)

Editor's Note:
Direct quotations, noted in red type, appear on the following pages:

Pages 9, 10, 11, 12, 17, 24 (panel 1), and 27 from *Manhunt: The 12-Day Chase for Lincoln's Killer* by James L. Swanson (New York: Harper Perennial, 2007).

Page 24 (panel 2) from "Testimony of Sergt. Boston Corbett" *New York Times* (http://www.nytimes.com/1865/05/18/news/testimony-of-sergt-boston-corbett.html

Page 29 from "The Gettysburg Address" by Abraham Lincoln, Abraham Lincoln Online (http://www.abrahamlincolnonline.org/lincoln/speeches/gettysburg.htm).

EDITOR
Christopher L. Harbo

ART DIRECTOR
Nathan Gassman

DESIGNER
Ashlee Suker

PRODUCTION SPECIALIST
Jennifer Walker

COVER ARTIST
Dante Ginevra

Printed in the United States 5360

TABLE OF CONTENTS

INTRODUCING ...

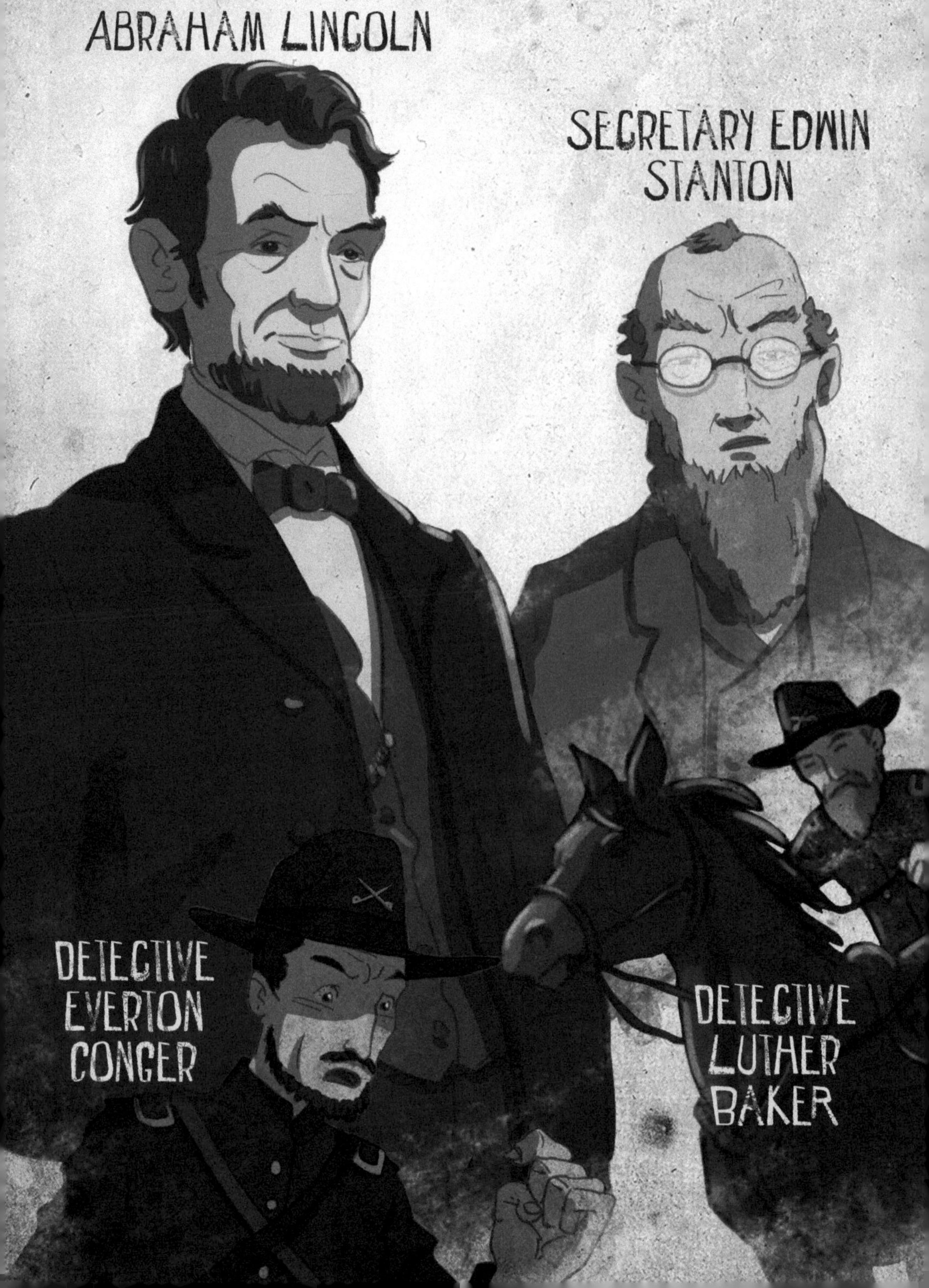
ABRAHAM LINCOLN
SECRETARY EDWIN STANTON
DETECTIVE EVERTON CONGER
DETECTIVE LUTHER BAKER

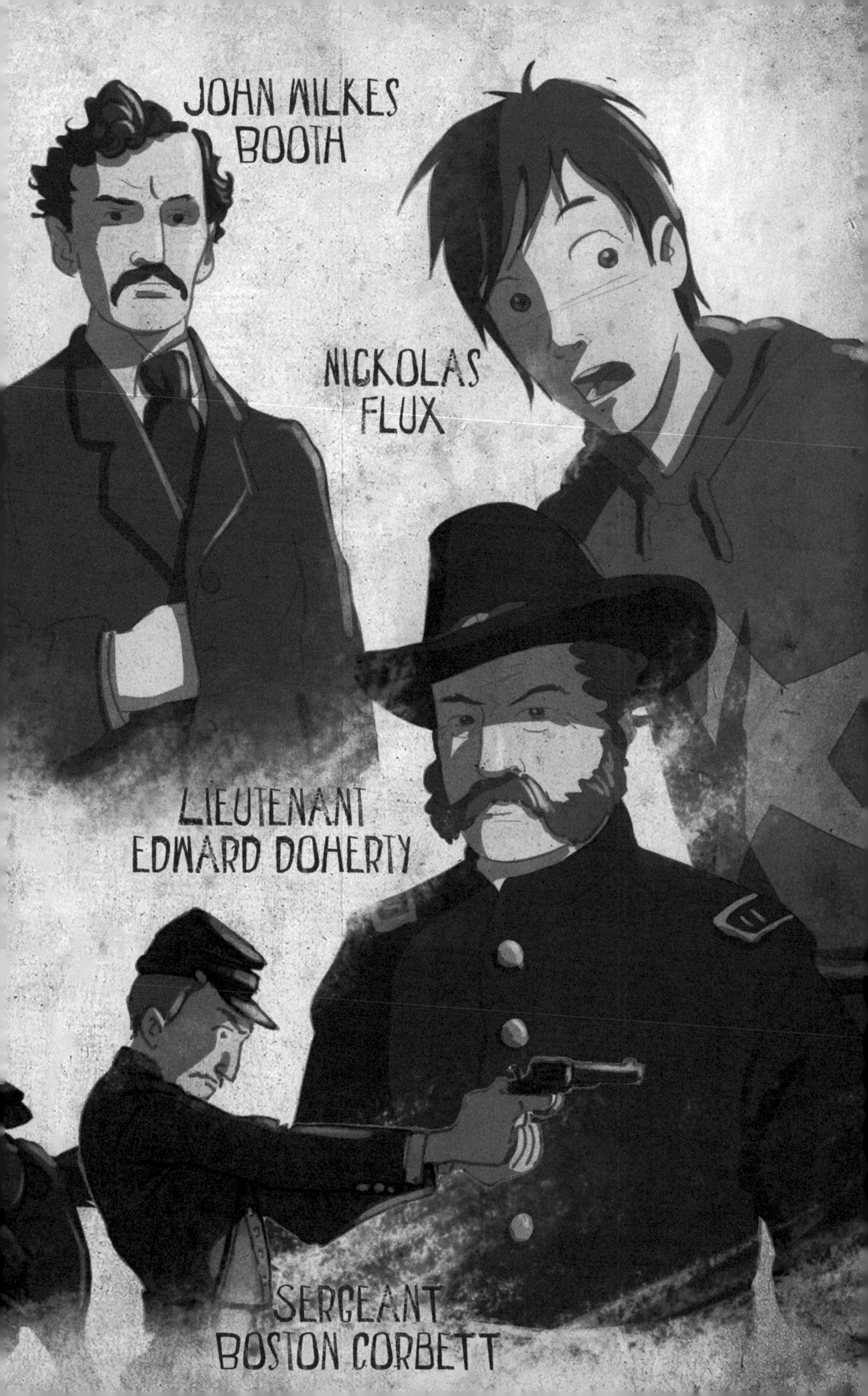
JOHN WILKES BOOTH
NICKOLAS FLUX
LIEUTENANT EDWARD DOHERTY
SERGEANT BOSTON CORBETT

CHAPTER ONE
BACKSTAGE JITTERS

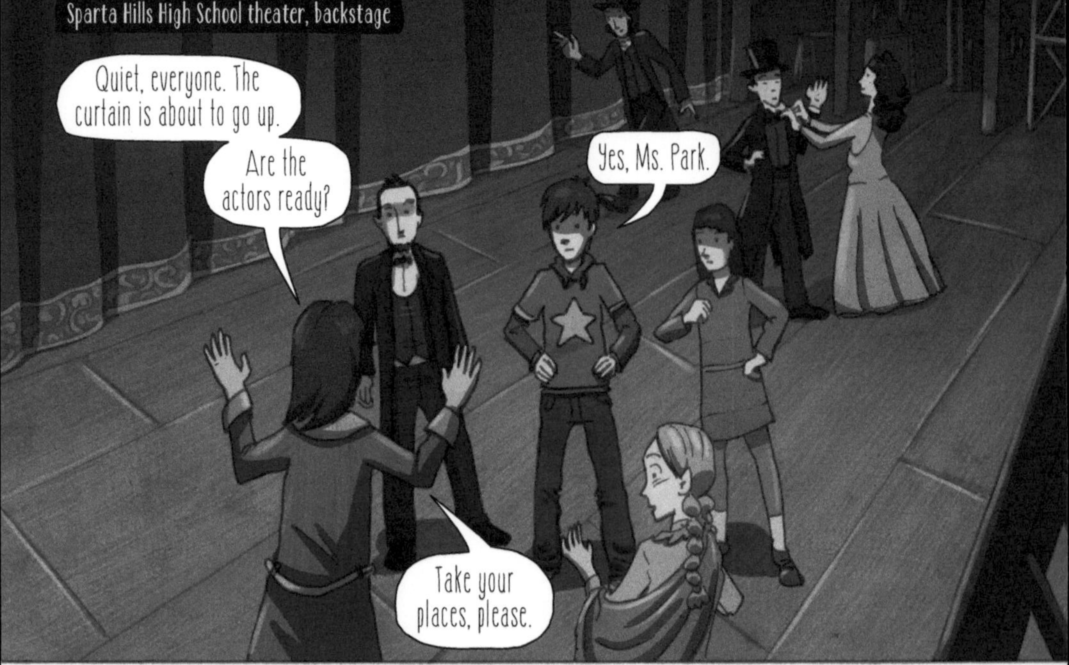
Sparta Hills High School theater, backstage
Quiet, everyone. The curtain is about to go up.
Are the actors ready?
Yes, Ms. Park.
Take your places, please.

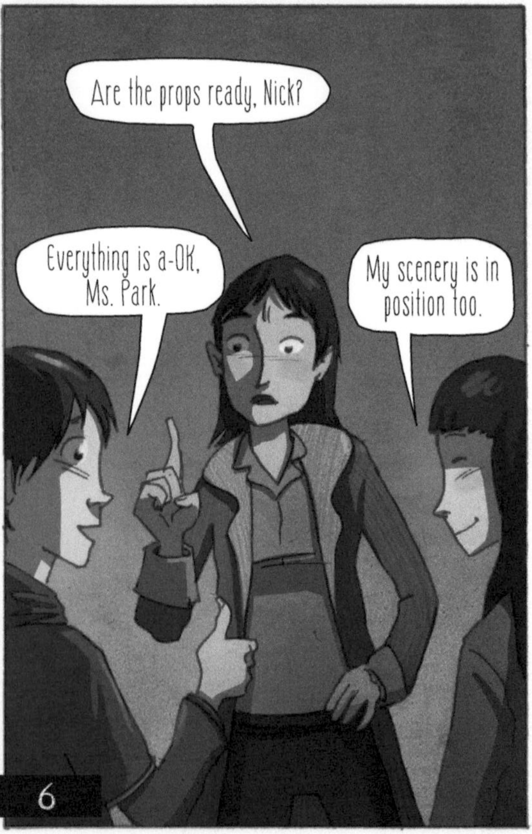
Are the props ready, Nick?
Everything is a-OK, Ms. Park.
My scenery is in position too.

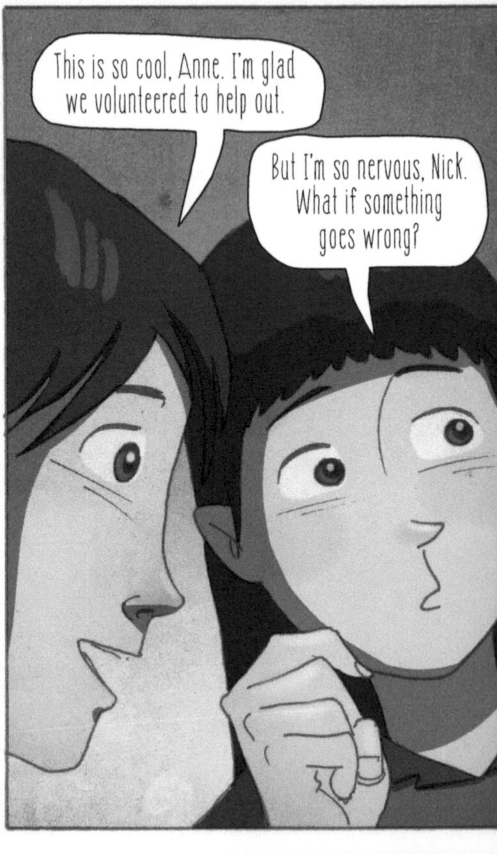
This is so cool, Anne. I'm glad we volunteered to help out.
But I'm so nervous, Nick. What if something goes wrong?

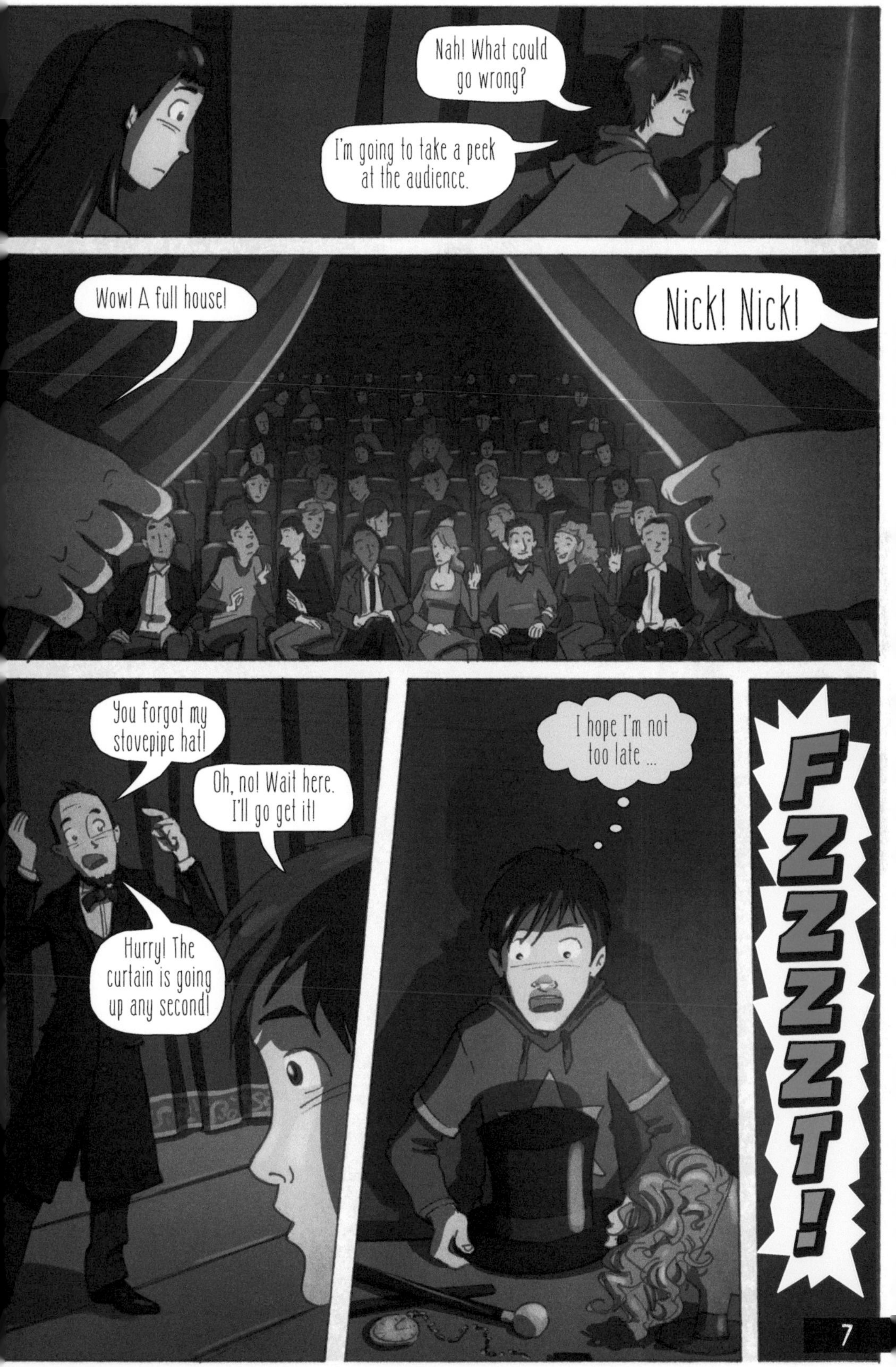

Nah! What could go wrong?
I'm going to take a peek at the audience.
Wow! A full house!
Nick! Nick!
You forgot my stovepipe hat!
Oh, no! Wait here. I'll go get it!
Hurry! The curtain is going up any second!
I hope I'm not too late ...
FZZZZT!

CHAPTER TWO
"HE HAS SHOT THE PRESIDENT"

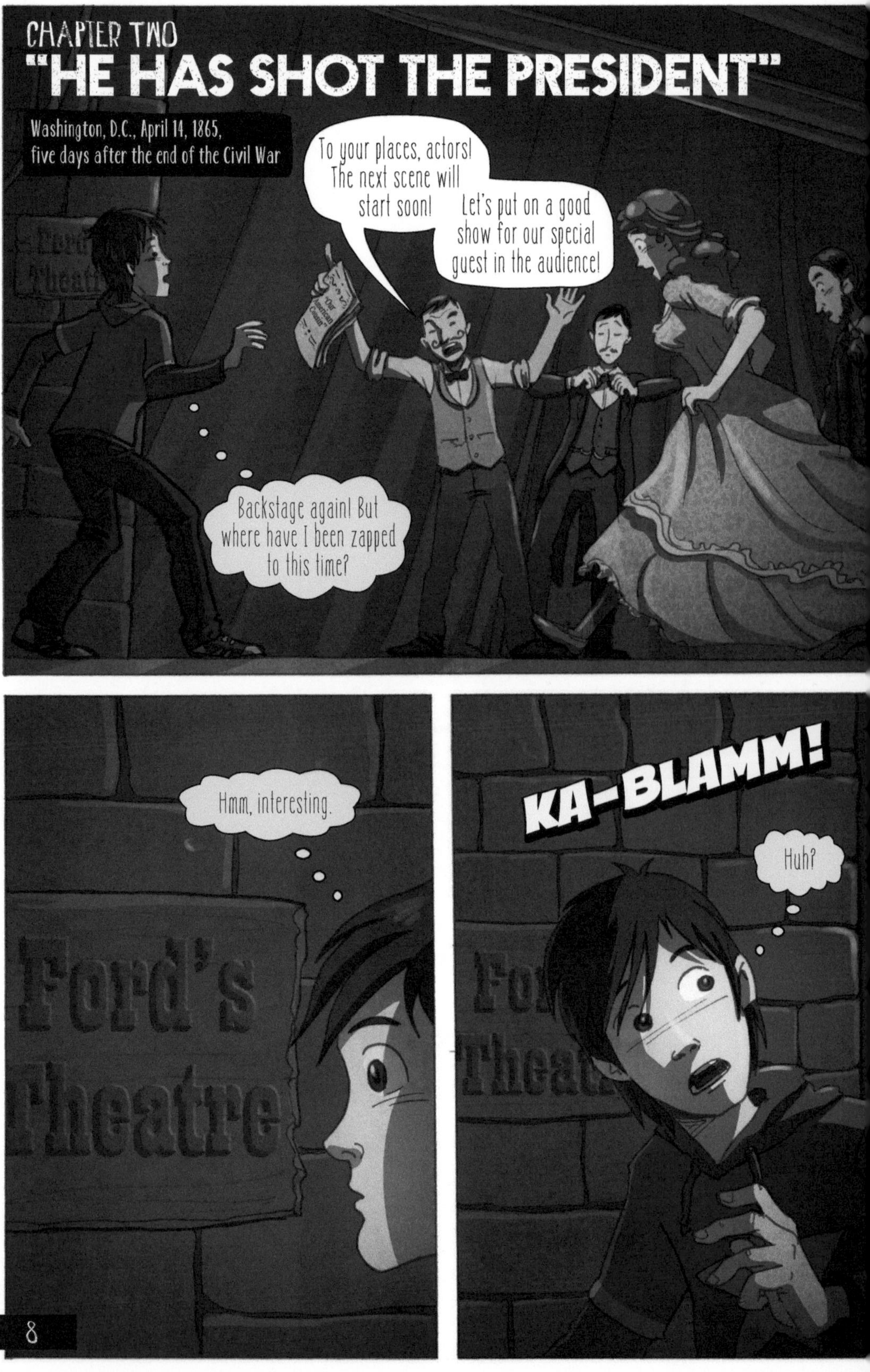

Washington, D.C., April 14, 1865, five days after the end of the Civil War
To your places, actors! The next scene will start soon!
Let's put on a good show for our special guest in the audience!
Backstage again! But where have I been zapped to this time?
Hmm, interesting.
Ford's Theatre
KA-BLAMM!
Huh?

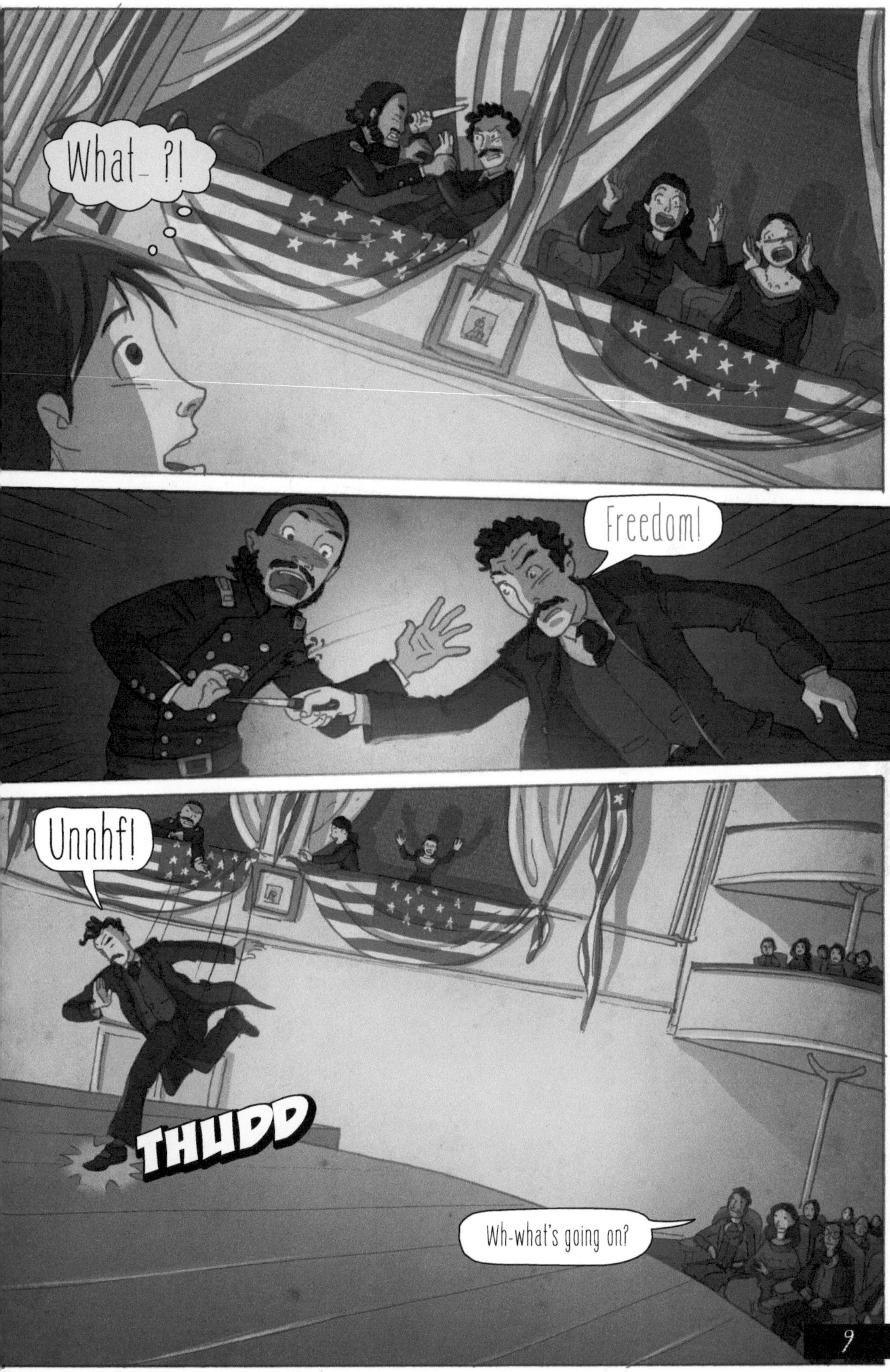

What– ?!
Freedom!
Unnhf!
THUDD
Wh-what's going on?

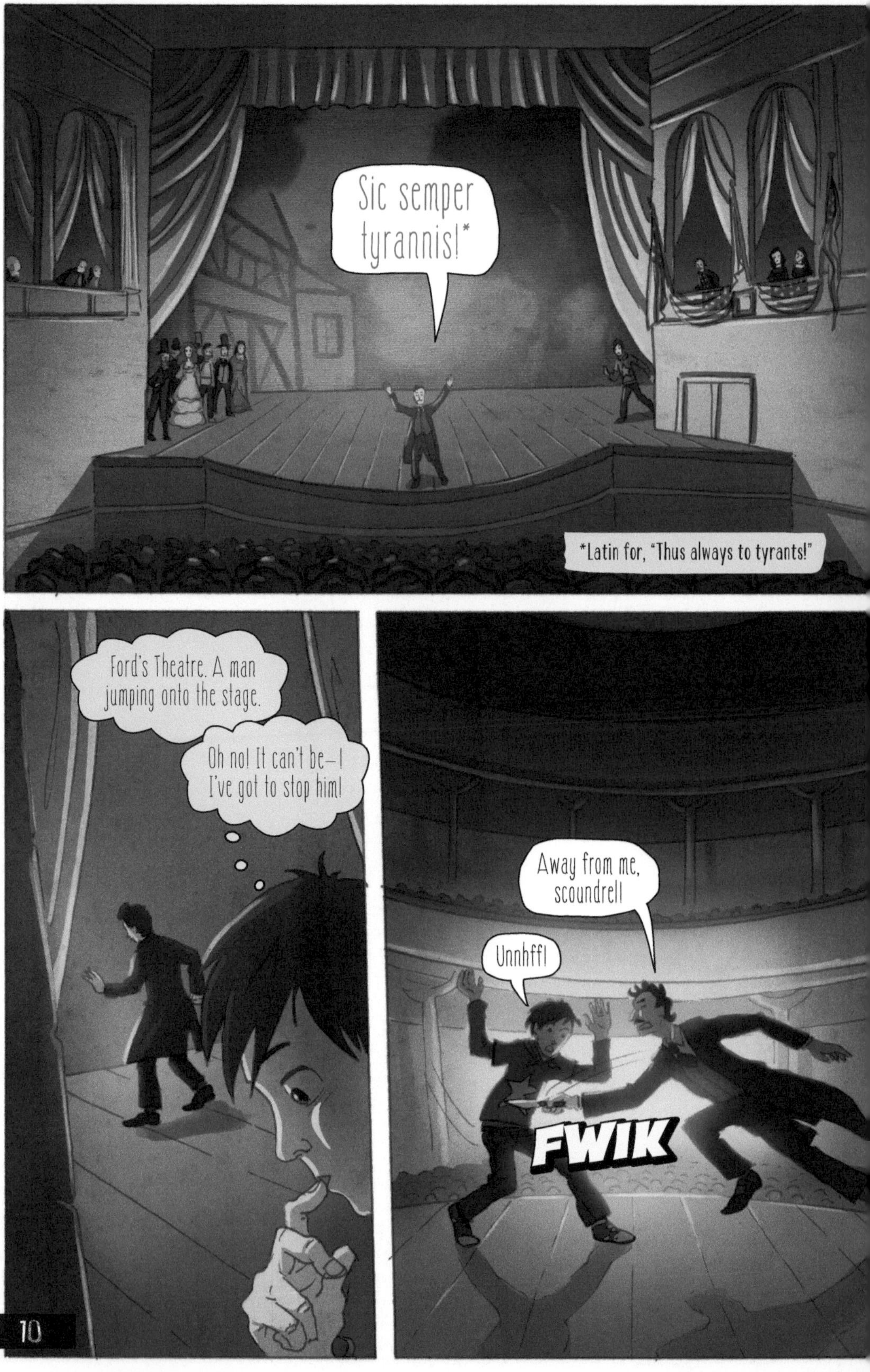
Sic semper tyrannis!*
*Latin for, "Thus always to tyrants!"
Ford's Theatre. A man jumping onto the stage.
Oh no! It can't be—I I've got to stop him!
Away from me, scoundrel!
Unnhff!
FWIK

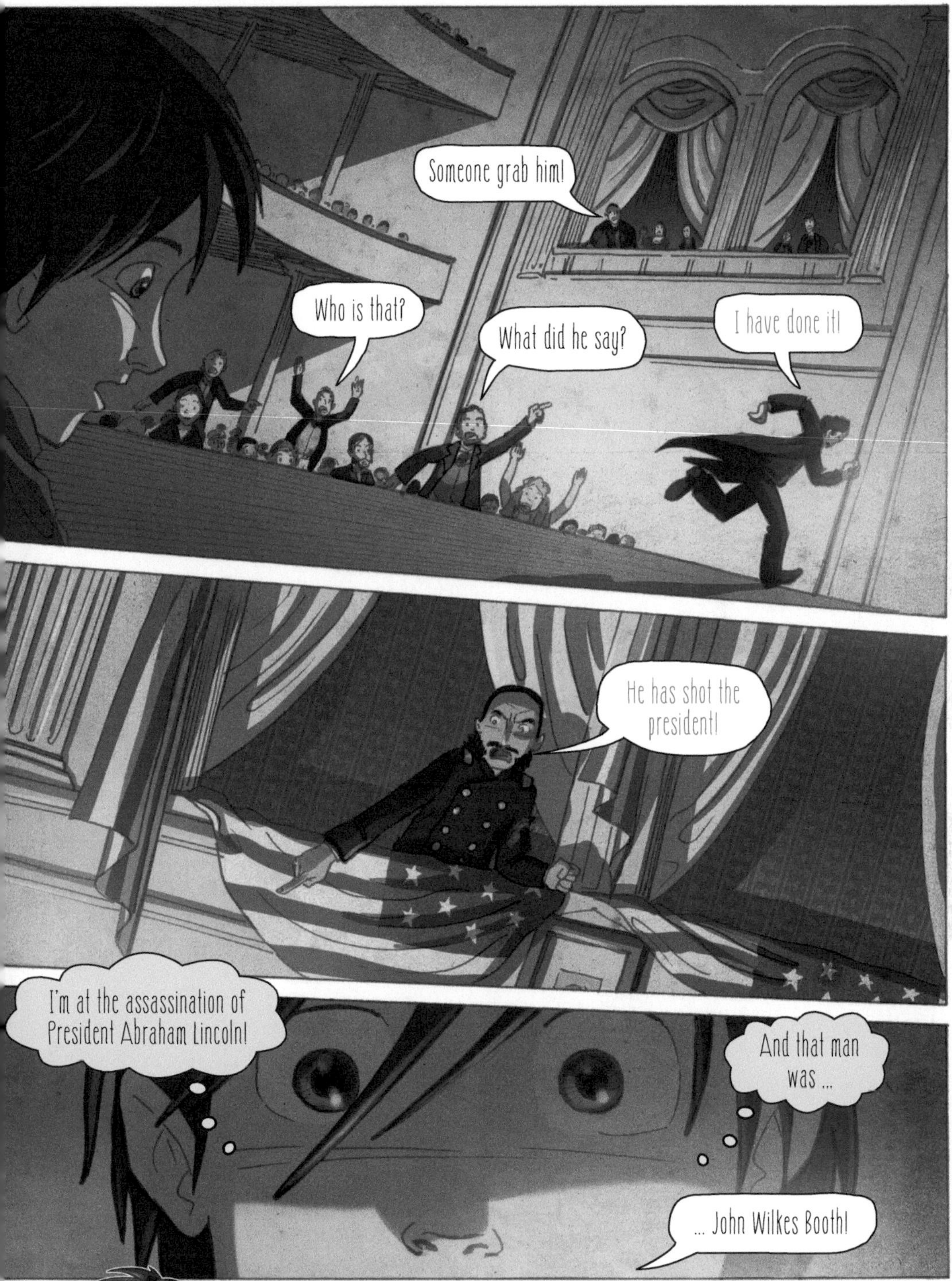
Someone grab him!
Who is that?
What did he say?
I have done it!
He has shot the president!
I'm at the assassination of President Abraham Lincoln!
And that man was ...
... John Wilkes Booth!

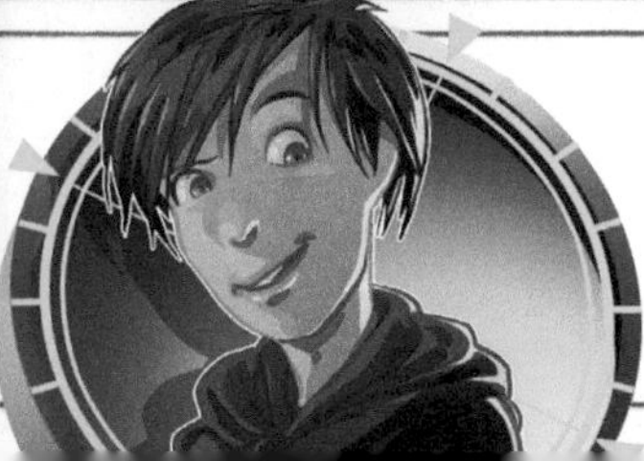

FLUX FACT

Booth was a famous actor and well known at Ford's Theatre. He knew the play being performed that night. He fired his shot during a scene he knew would make the audience laugh to muffle the sound.

CHAPTER THREE
"HIS WOUND IS MORTAL"

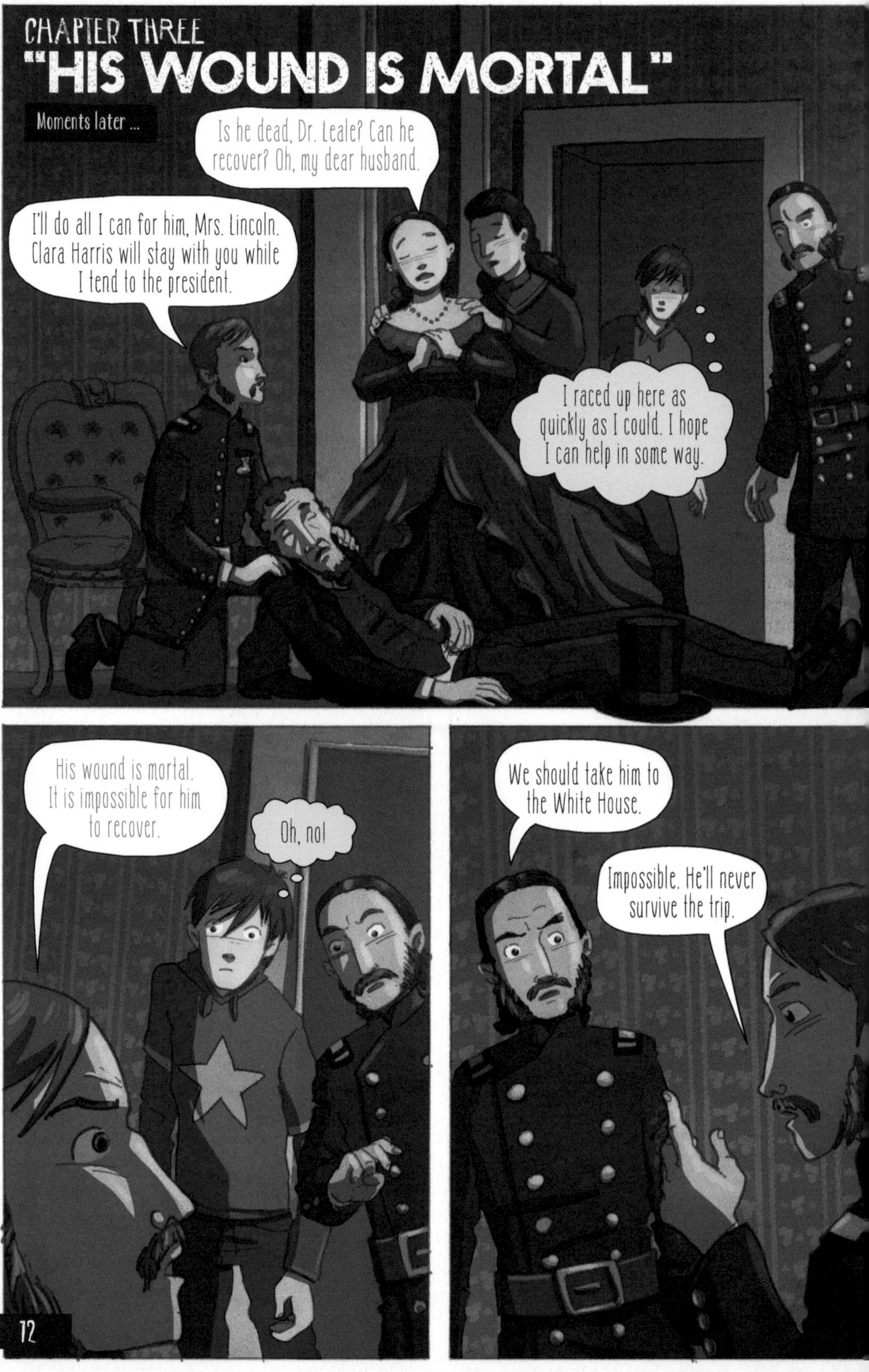
Moments later ...
Is he dead, Dr. Leale? Can he recover? Oh, my dear husband.
I'll do all I can for him, Mrs. Lincoln. Clara Harris will stay with you while I tend to the president.
I raced up here as quickly as I could. I hope I can help in some way.
His wound is mortal. It is impossible for him to recover.
Oh, no!
We should take him to the White House.
Impossible. He'll never survive the trip.

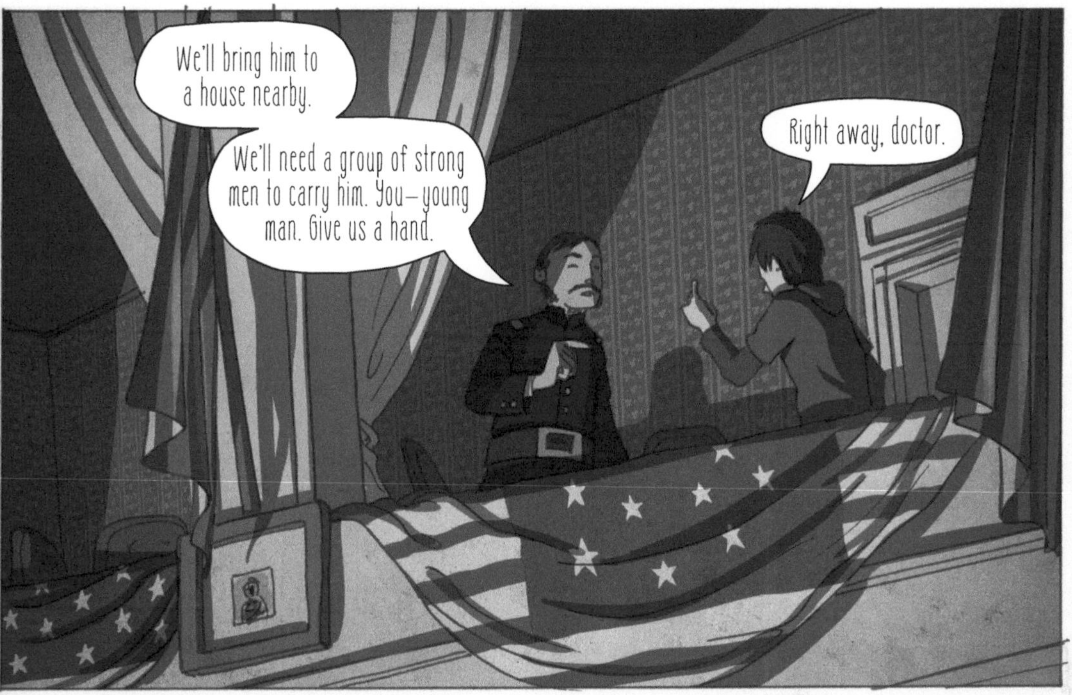
We'll bring him to a house nearby.
We'll need a group of strong men to carry him. You—young man. Give us a hand.
Right away, doctor.

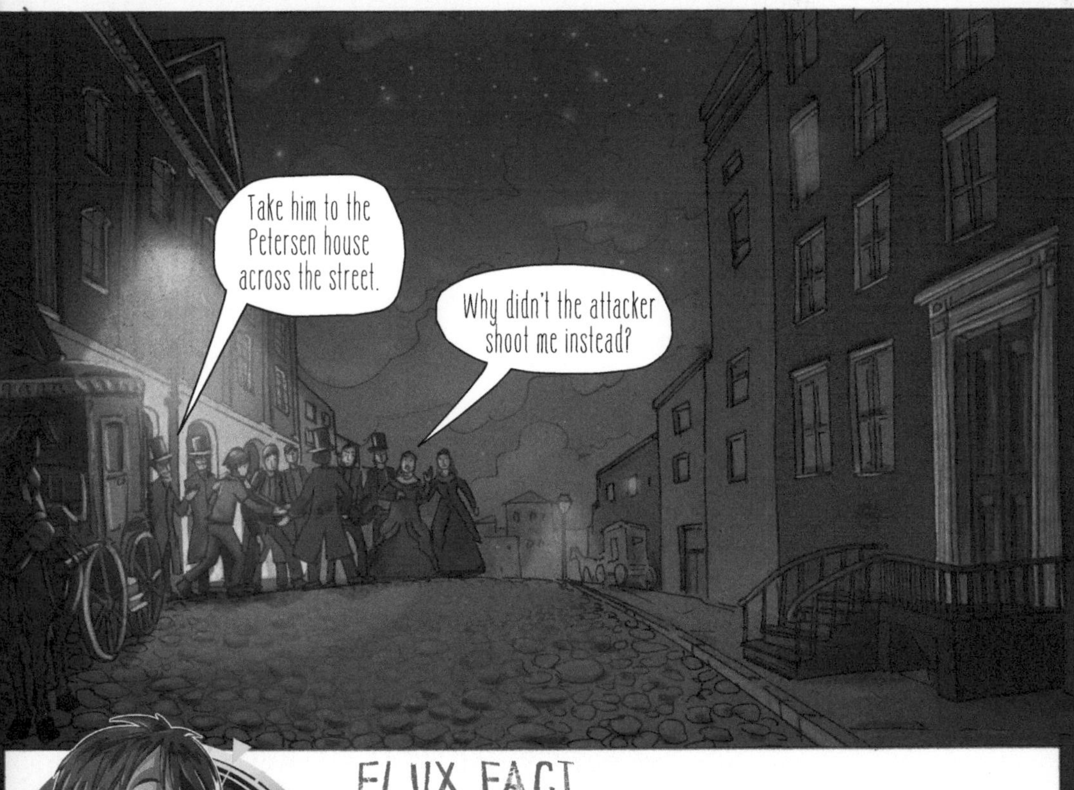
Take him to the Petersen house across the street.
Why didn't the attacker shoot me instead?

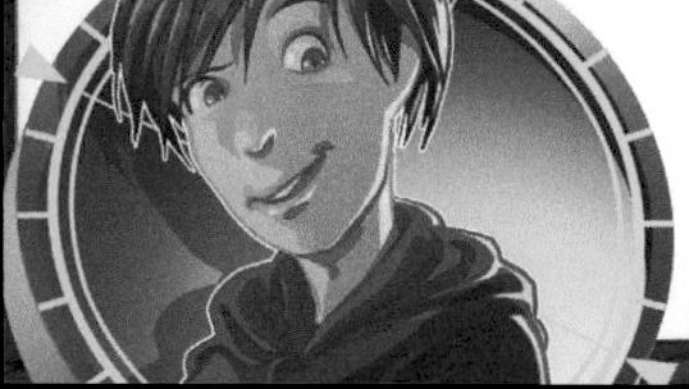

FLUX FACT

Dr. Charles Leale was a surgeon in the Union Army during the Civil War. He was in the audience the night of the shooting. He was the first of several doctors to arrive in the presidential box.

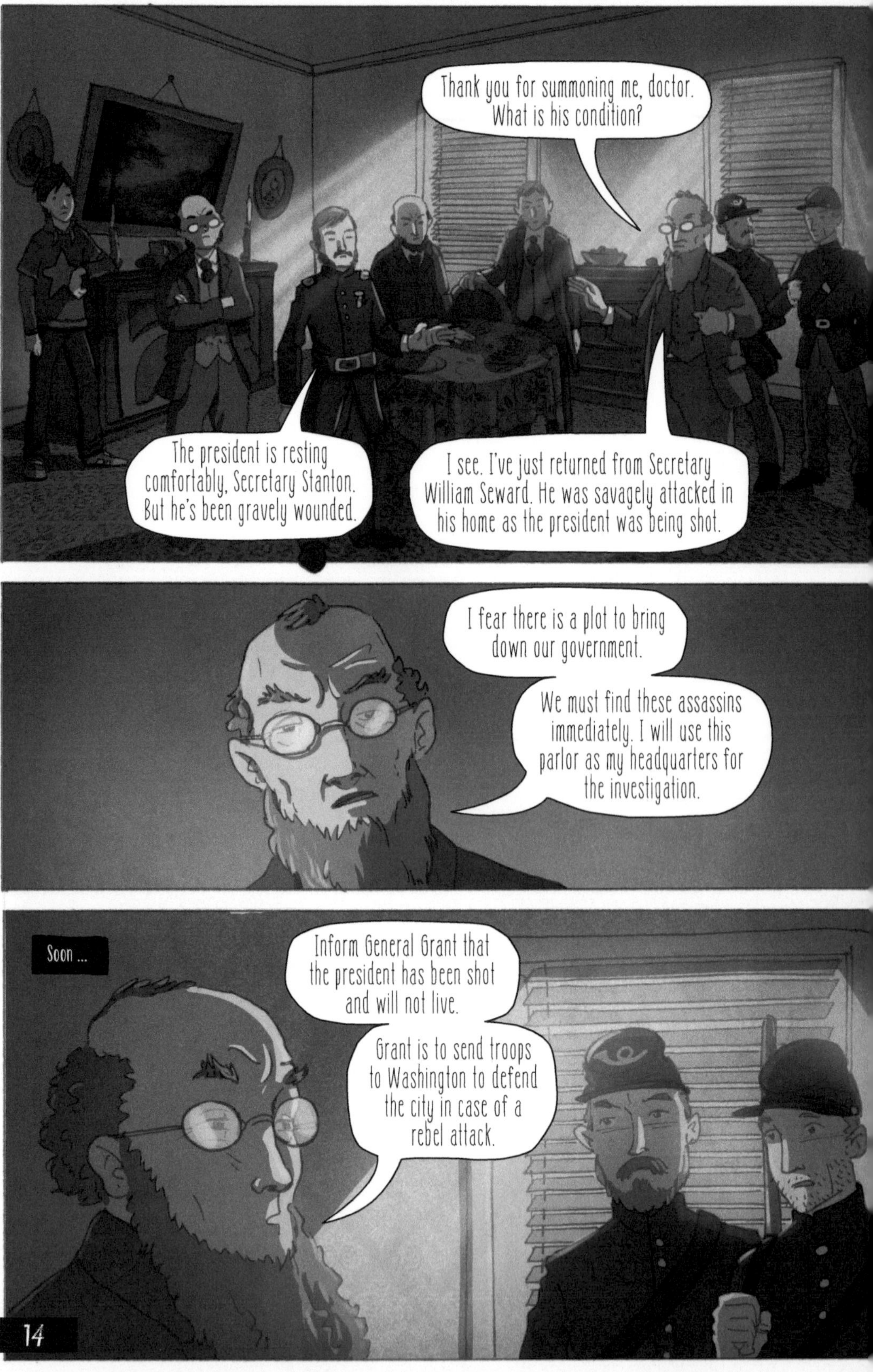
Thank you for summoning me, doctor. What is his condition?
The president is resting comfortably, Secretary Stanton. But he's been gravely wounded.
I see. I've just returned from Secretary William Seward. He was savagely attacked in his home as the president was being shot.
I fear there is a plot to bring down our government.
We must find these assassins immediately. I will use this parlor as my headquarters for the investigation.
Soon ...
Inform General Grant that the president has been shot and will not live.
Grant is to send troops to Washington to defend the city in case of a rebel attack.

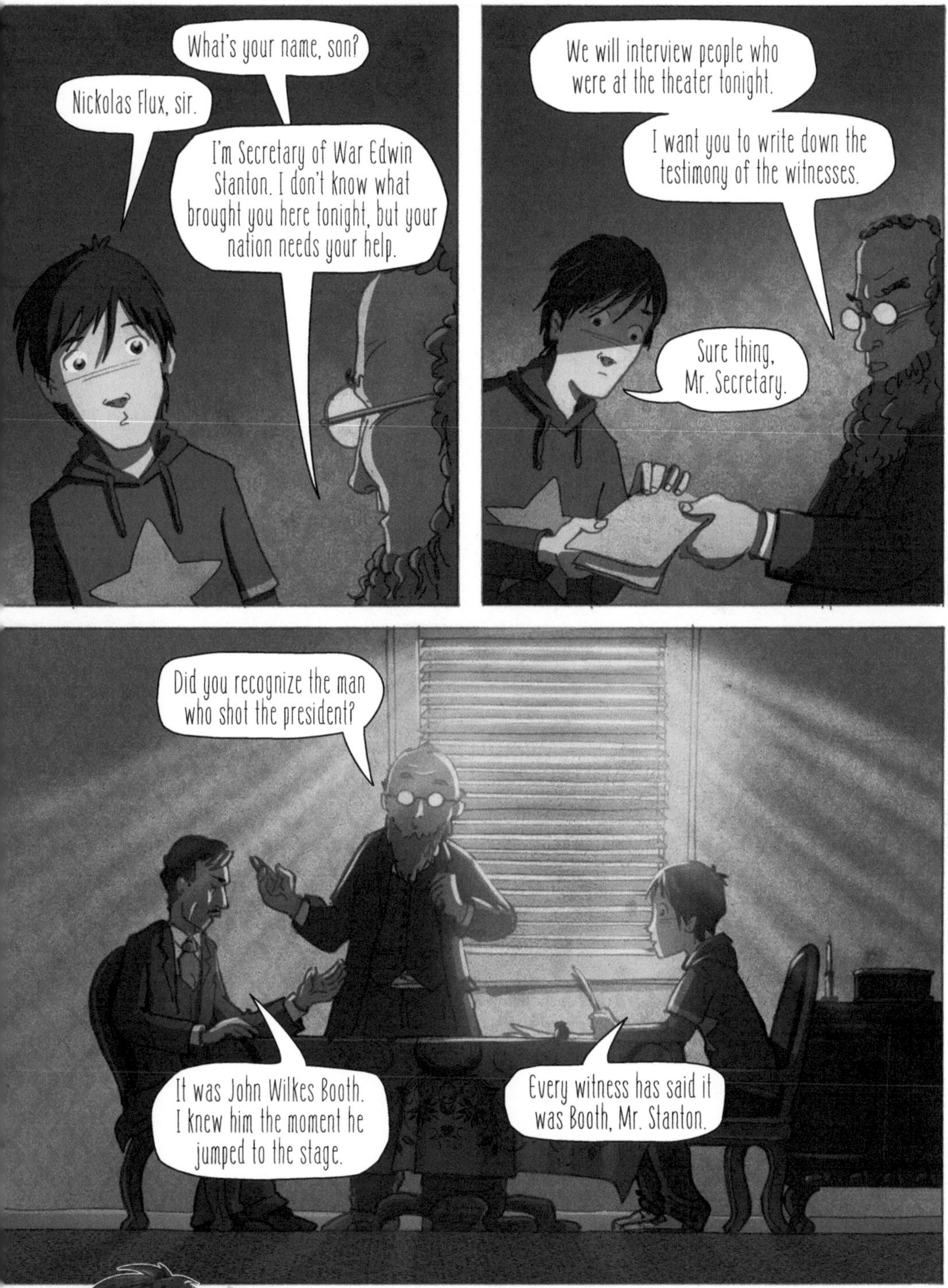
What's your name, son?
Nickolas Flux, sir.
I'm Secretary of War Edwin Stanton. I don't know what brought you here tonight, but your nation needs your help.
We will interview people who were at the theater tonight.
I want you to write down the testimony of the witnesses.
Sure thing, Mr. Secretary.
Did you recognize the man who shot the president?
It was John Wilkes Booth. I knew him the moment he jumped to the stage.
Every witness has said it was Booth, Mr. Stanton.

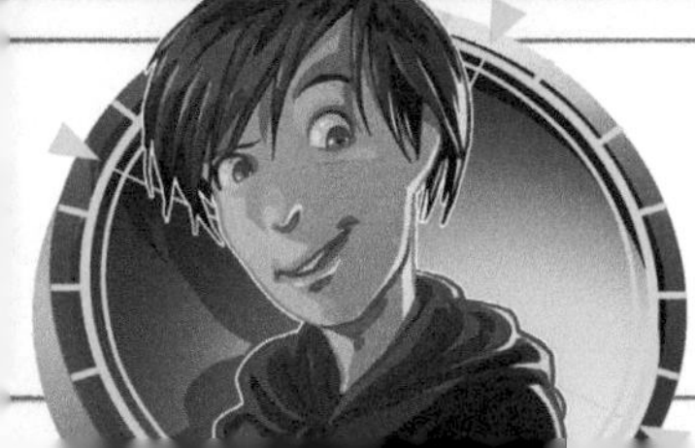

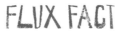

FLUX FACT

Secretary of War Edwin Stanton served under Lincoln during the Civil War. He organized the Union's war efforts and helped guide the Union to victory.

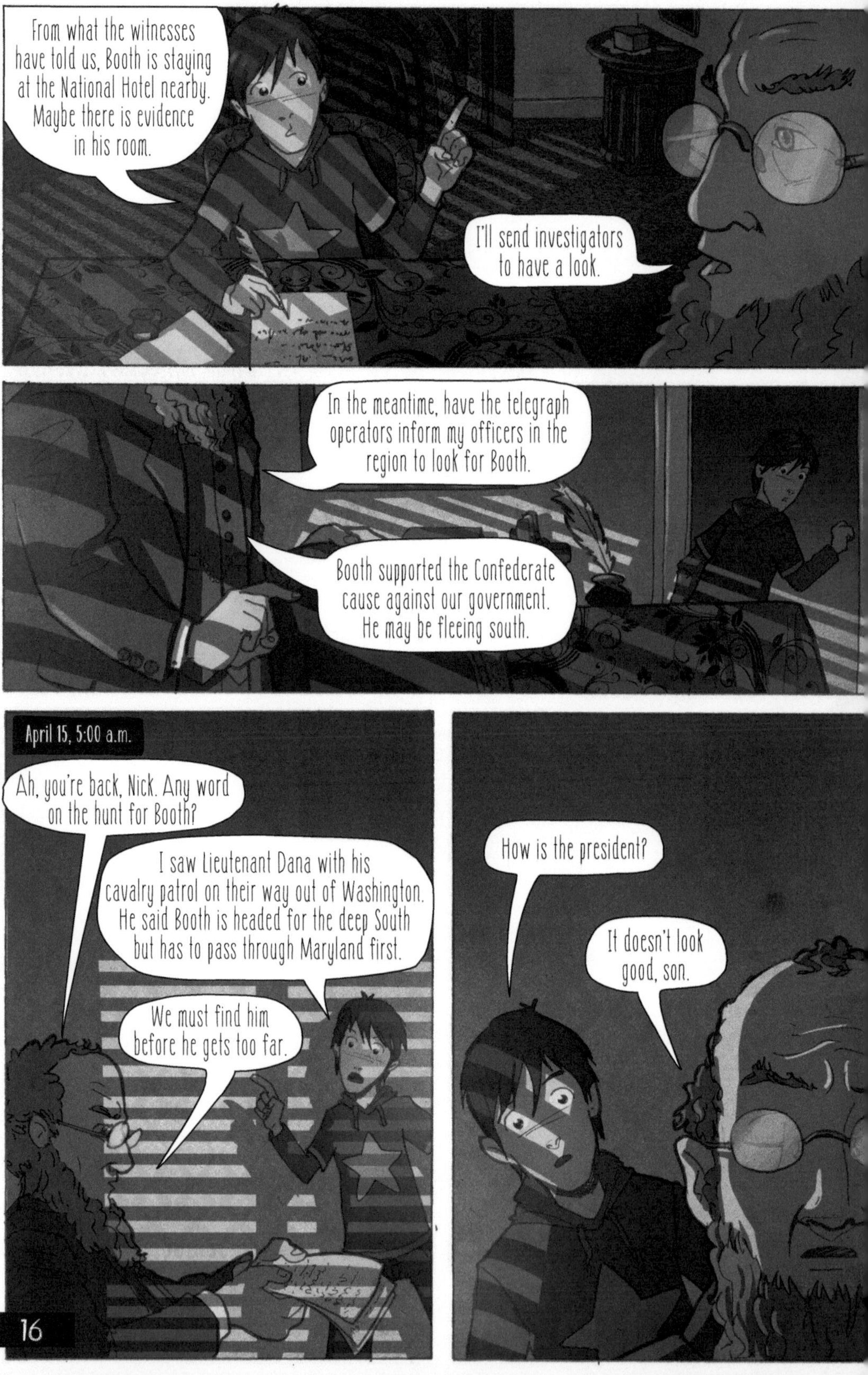
From what the witnesses have told us, Booth is staying at the National Hotel nearby. Maybe there is evidence in his room.
I'll send investigators to have a look.
In the meantime, have the telegraph operators inform my officers in the region to look for Booth.
Booth supported the Confederate cause against our government. He may be fleeing south.
April 15, 5:00 a.m.
Ah, you're back, Nick. Any word on the hunt for Booth?
I saw Lieutenant Dana with his cavalry patrol on their way out of Washington. He said Booth is headed for the deep South but has to pass through Maryland first.
We must find him before he gets too far.
How is the president?
It doesn't look good, son.

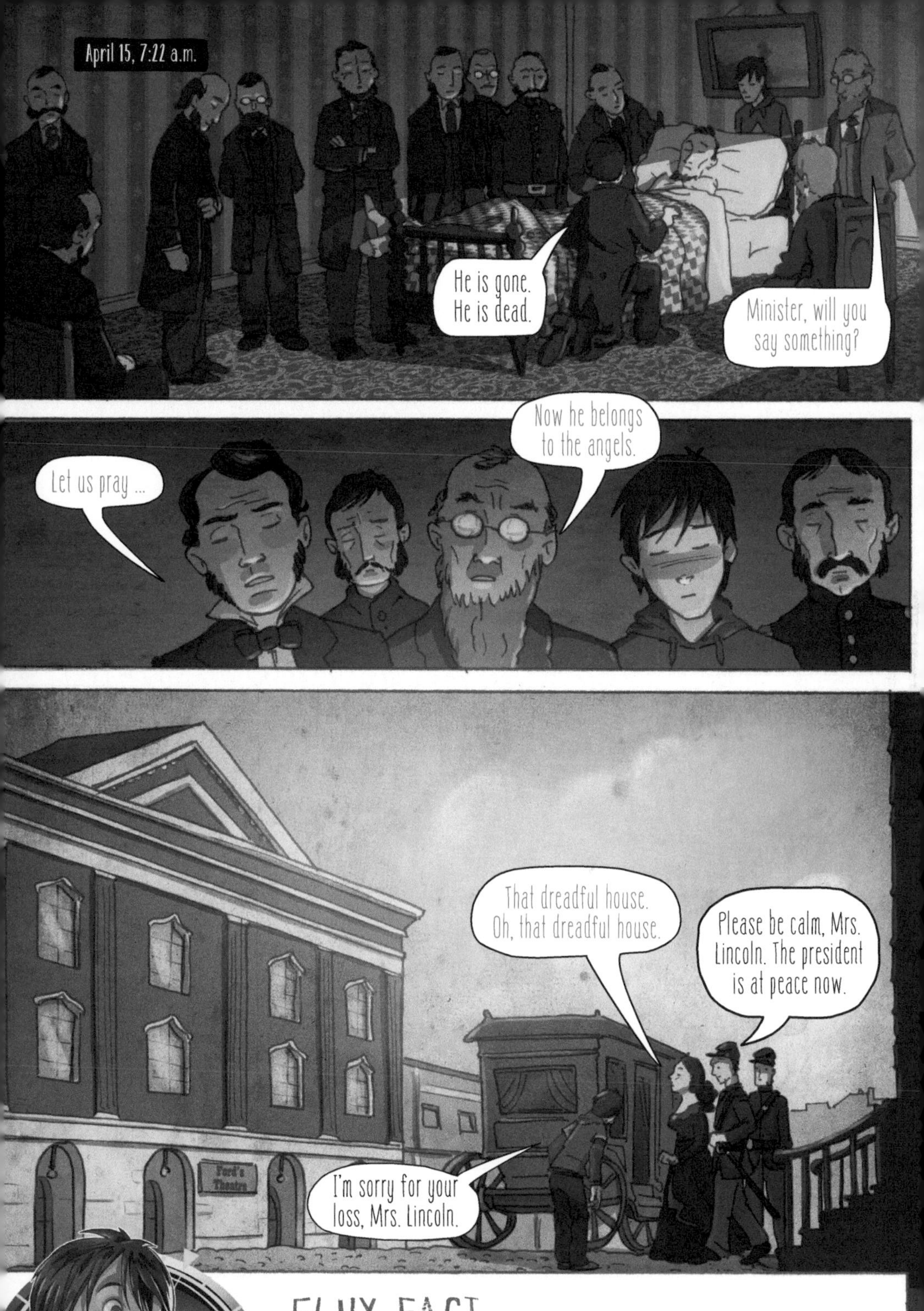
April 15, 7:22 a.m.
He is gone. He is dead.
Minister, will you say something?
Let us pray ...
Now he belongs to the angels.
That dreadful house. Oh, that dreadful house.
Please be calm, Mrs. Lincoln. The president is at peace now.
Ford's Theatre
I'm sorry for your loss, Mrs. Lincoln.

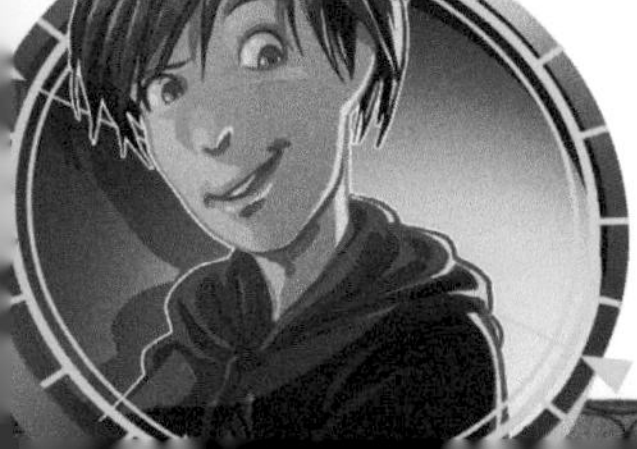

FLUX FACT

A letter written by someone named "Sam" was found in Booth's room at the National Hotel. It led investigators to believe that many people—not only Booth—were involved in the plot to assassinate Lincoln.

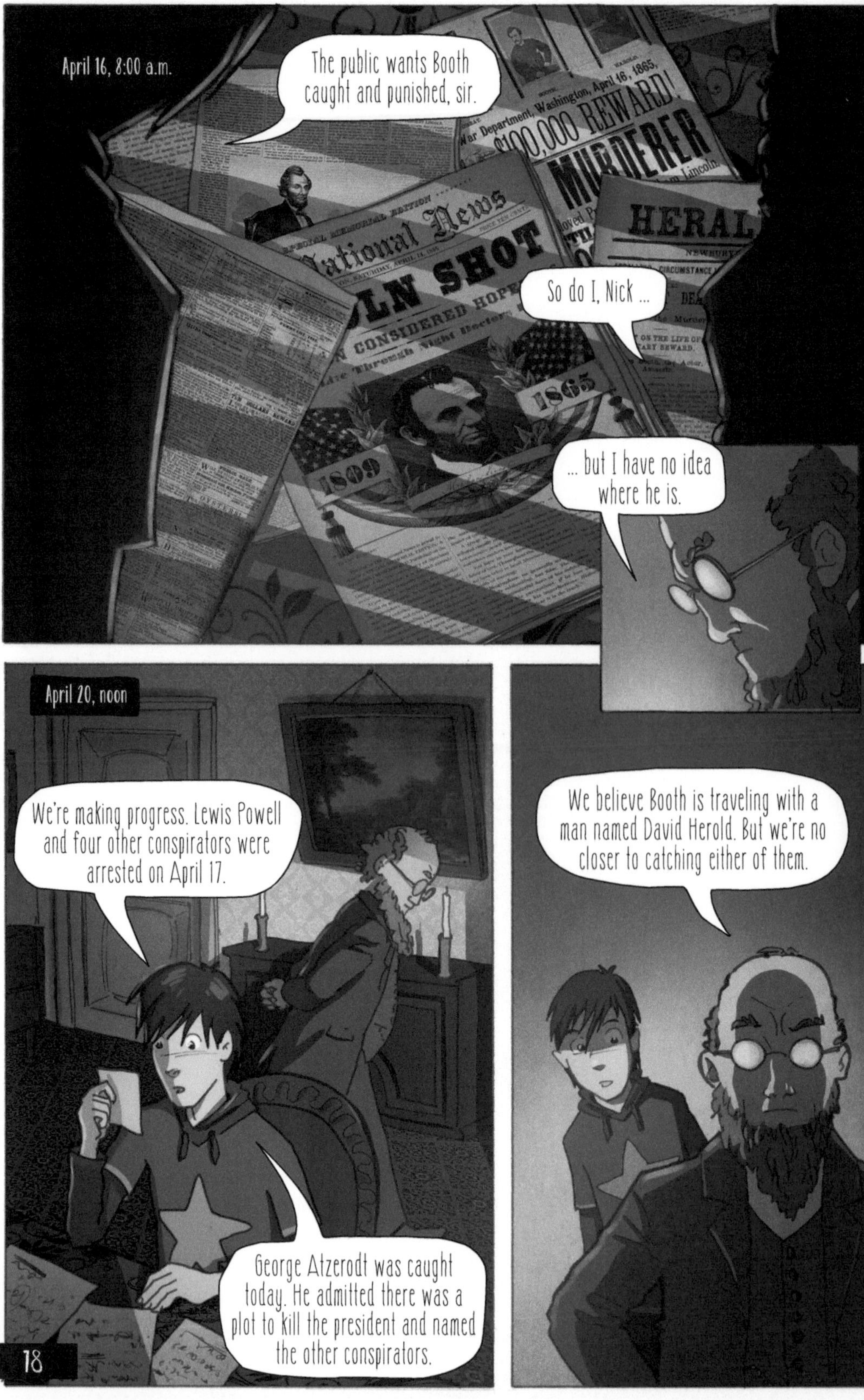
April 16, 8:00 a.m.
The public wants Booth caught and punished, sir.
War Department, Washington, April 16, 1865,
$100,000 REWARD!
MURDERER
National News
HERAL
1865
1809
So do I, Nick ...
... but I have no idea where he is.
April 20, noon
We're making progress. Lewis Powell and four other conspirators were arrested on April 17.
George Atzerodt was caught today. He admitted there was a plot to kill the president and named the other conspirators.
We believe Booth is traveling with a man named David Herold. But we're no closer to catching either of them.

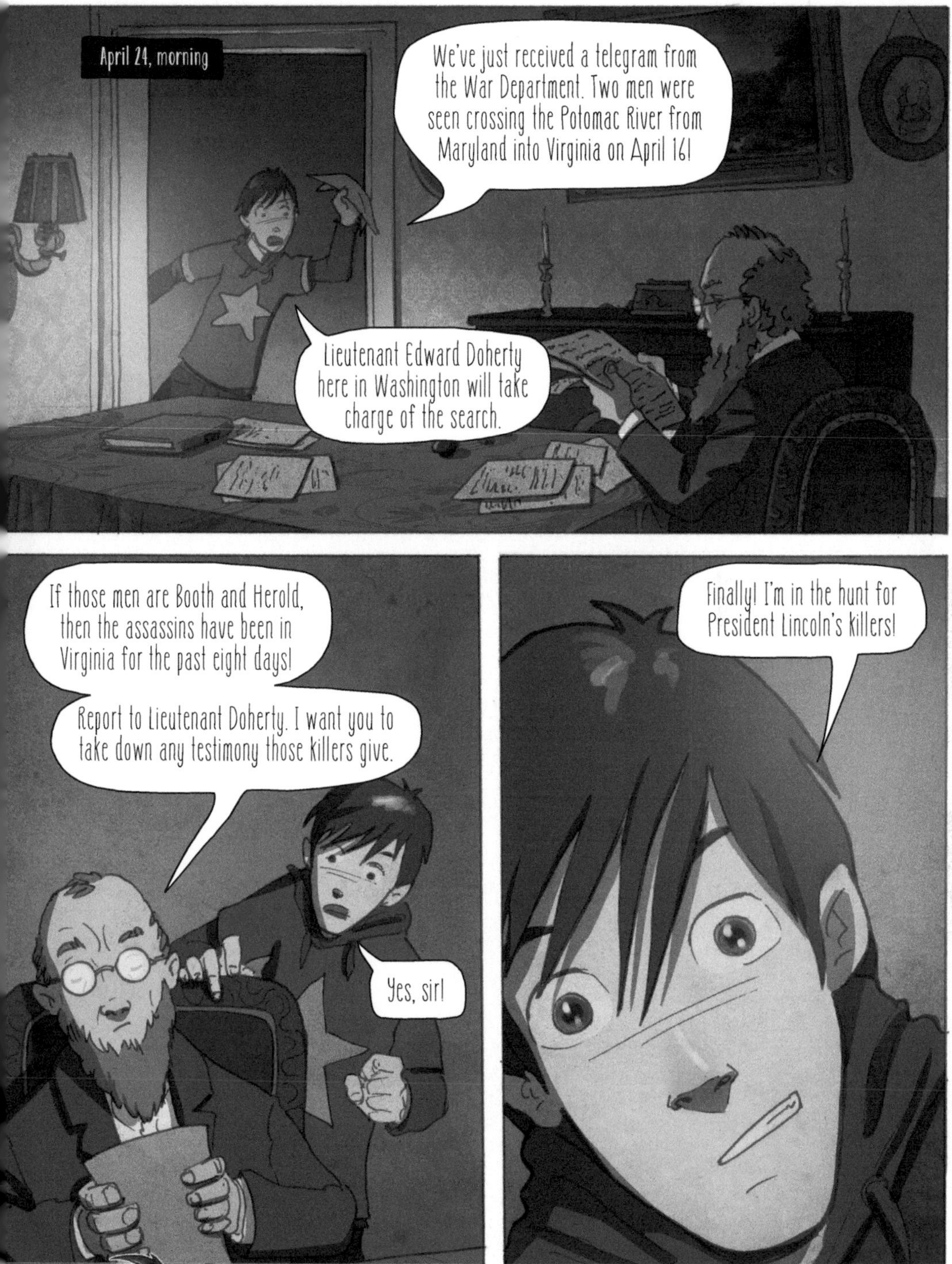
April 24, morning
We've just received a telegram from the War Department. Two men were seen crossing the Potomac River from Maryland into Virginia on April 16!
Lieutenant Edward Doherty here in Washington will take charge of the search.
If those men are Booth and Herold, then the assassins have been in Virginia for the past eight days!
Report to Lieutenant Doherty. I want you to take down any testimony those killers give.
Yes, sir!
Finally! I'm in the hunt for President Lincoln's killers!

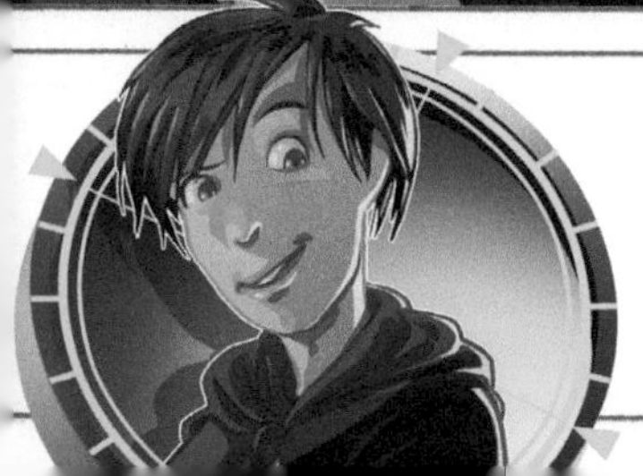

FLUX FACT

Two men had been seen crossing the Potomac River on April 16. It turned out they weren't John Wilkes Booth and David Herold. But the false alarm helped put the authorities on Booth's trail.

CHAPTER FOUR
TRAPPED!

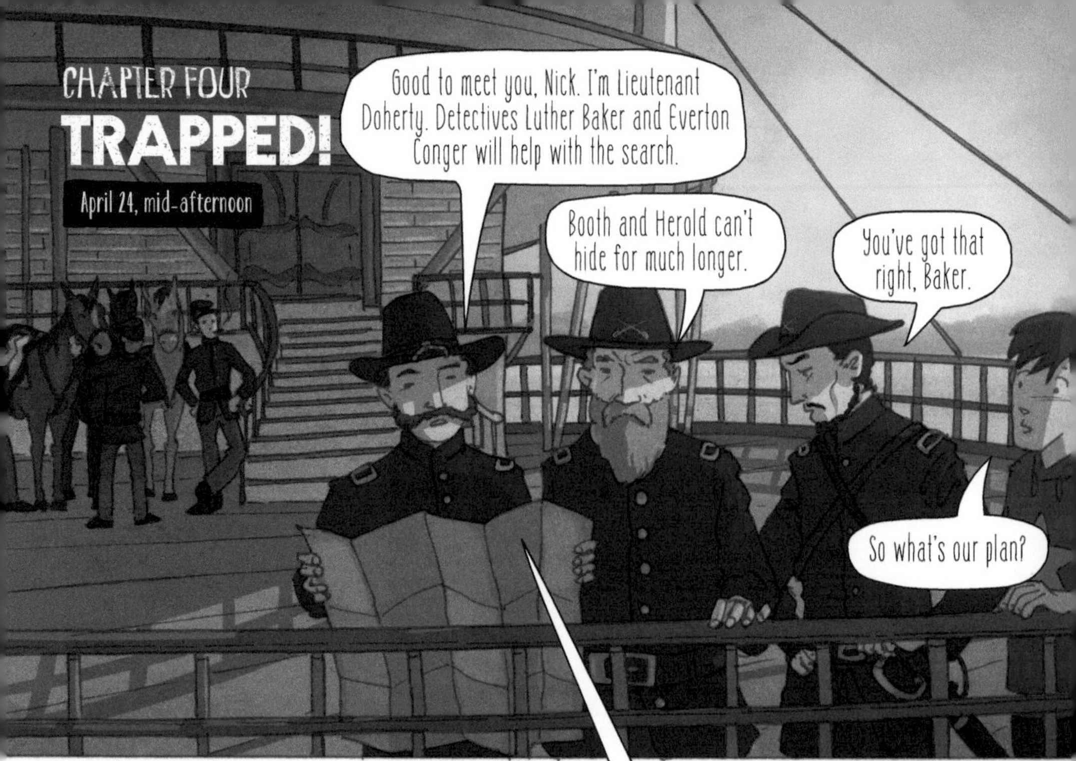
April 24, mid-afternoon
Good to meet you, Nick. I'm Lieutenant Doherty. Detectives Luther Baker and Everton Conger will help with the search.
Booth and Herold can't hide for much longer.
You've got that right, Baker.
So what's our plan?

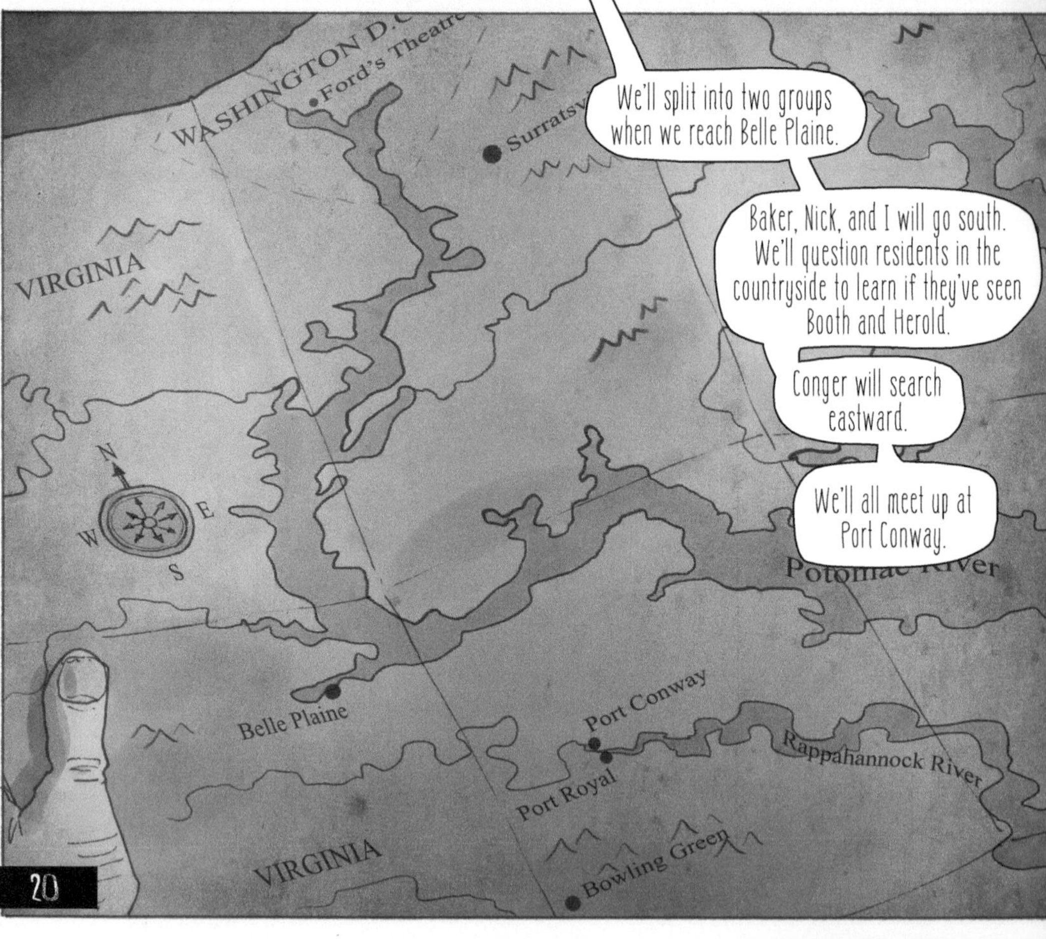
We'll split into two groups when we reach Belle Plaine.
Baker, Nick, and I will go south. We'll question residents in the countryside to learn if they've seen Booth and Herold.
Conger will search eastward.
We'll all meet up at Port Conway.
WASHINGTON D.C.
Ford's Theatre
VIRGINIA
N
E
W
S
Potomac River
Belle Plaine
Port Conway
Port Royal
Rappahannock River
VIRGINIA
Bowling Green

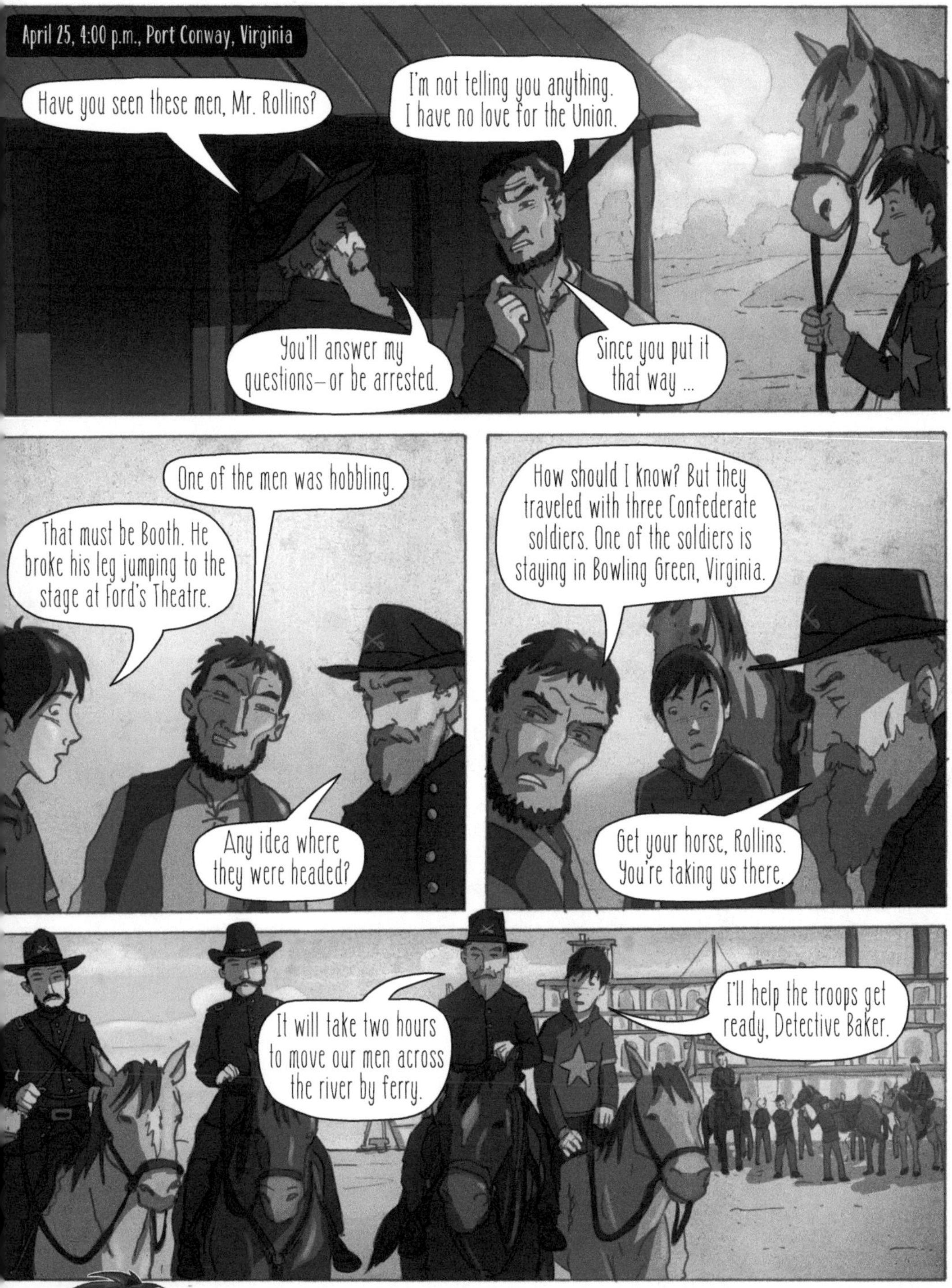
April 25, 4:00 p.m., Port Conway, Virginia
Have you seen these men, Mr. Rollins?
I'm not telling you anything. I have no love for the Union.
You'll answer my questions—or be arrested.
Since you put it that way ...
One of the men was hobbling.
That must be Booth. He broke his leg jumping to the stage at Ford's Theatre.
Any idea where they were headed?
How should I know? But they traveled with three Confederate soldiers. One of the soldiers is staying in Bowling Green, Virginia.
Get your horse, Rollins. You're taking us there.
It will take two hours to move our men across the river by ferry.
I'll help the troops get ready, Detective Baker.

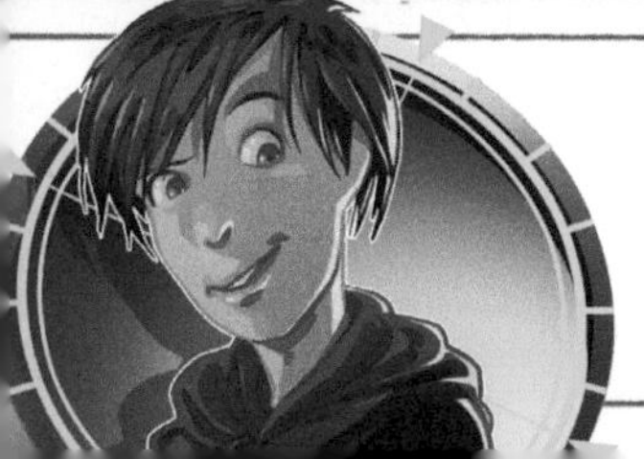

FLUX FACT

William Rollins fought for the Confederacy during the Civil War. He was not eager to help the Union soldiers on their manhunt. Detective Baker's threat to arrest him changed Rollins' mind.

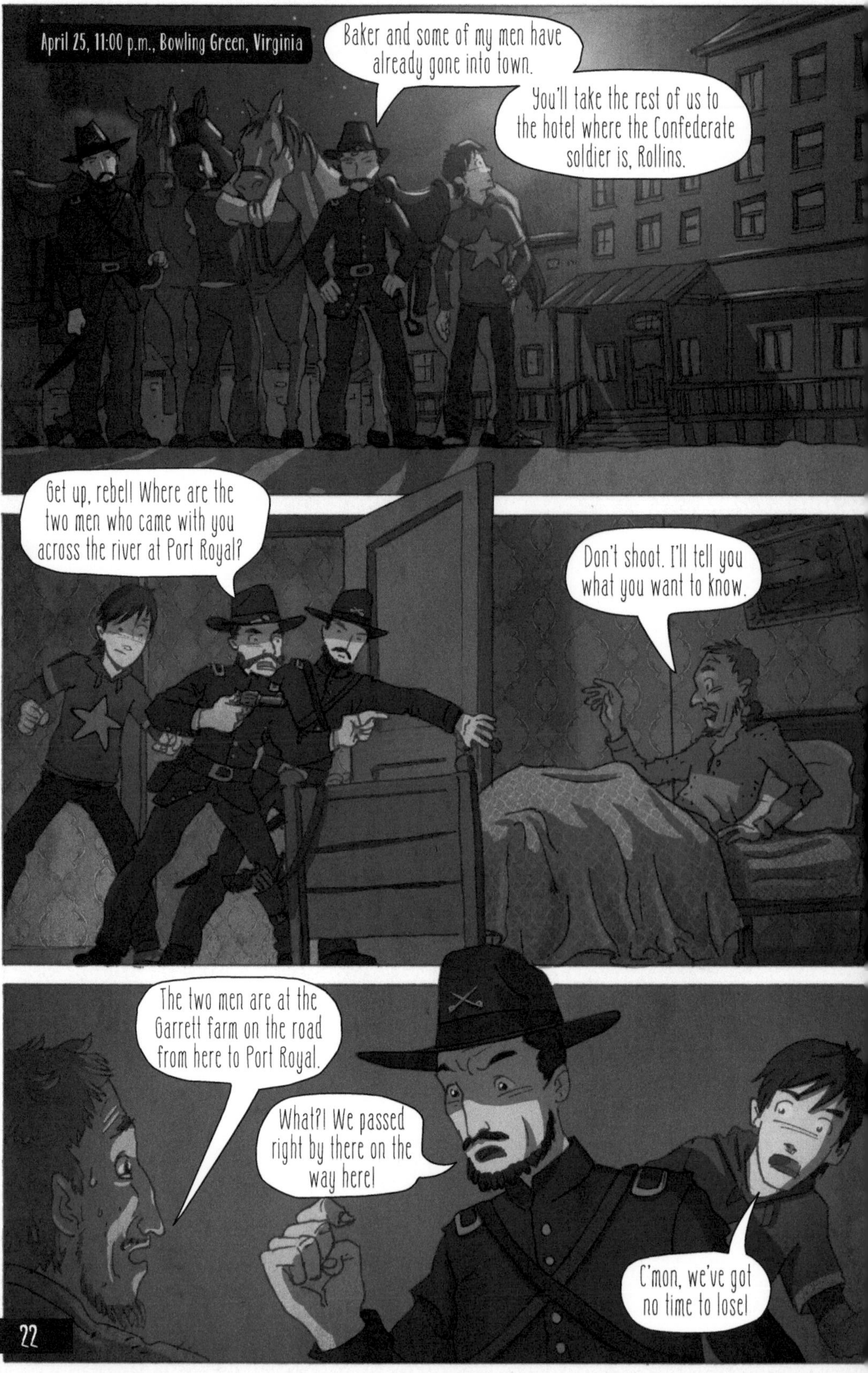
April 25, 11:00 p.m., Bowling Green, Virginia
Baker and some of my men have already gone into town.
You'll take the rest of us to the hotel where the Confederate soldier is, Rollins.
Get up, rebel! Where are the two men who came with you across the river at Port Royal?
Don't shoot. I'll tell you what you want to know.
The two men are at the Garrett farm on the road from here to Port Royal.
What?! We passed right by there on the way here!
C'mon, we've got no time to lose!

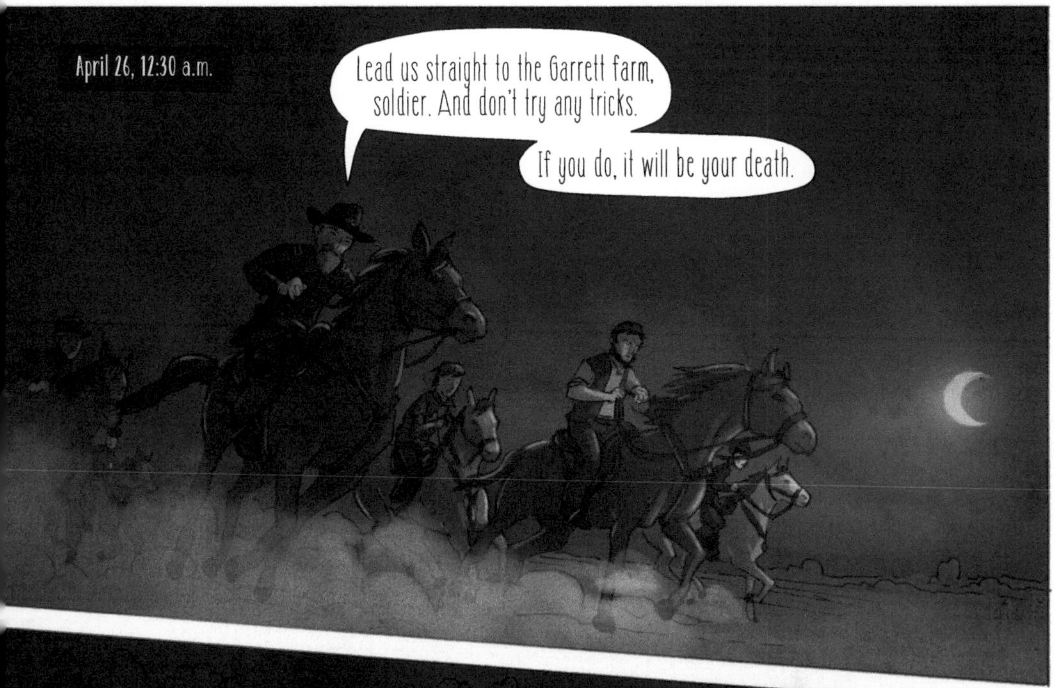
April 26, 12:30 a.m.
Lead us straight to the Garrett farm, soldier. And don't try any tricks.
If you do, it will be your death.

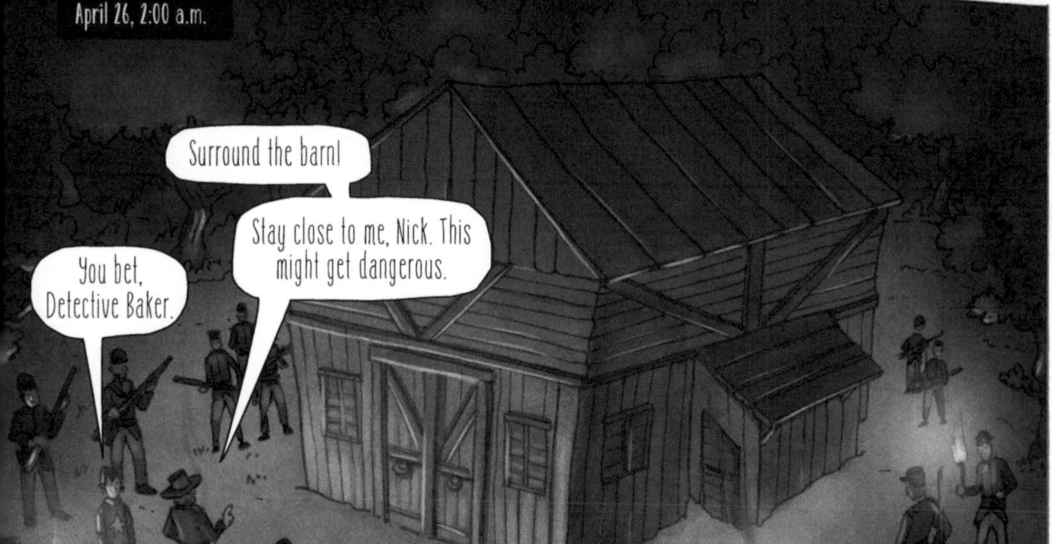
April 26, 2:00 a.m.
Surround the barn!
Stay close to me, Nick. This might get dangerous.
You bet, Detective Baker.

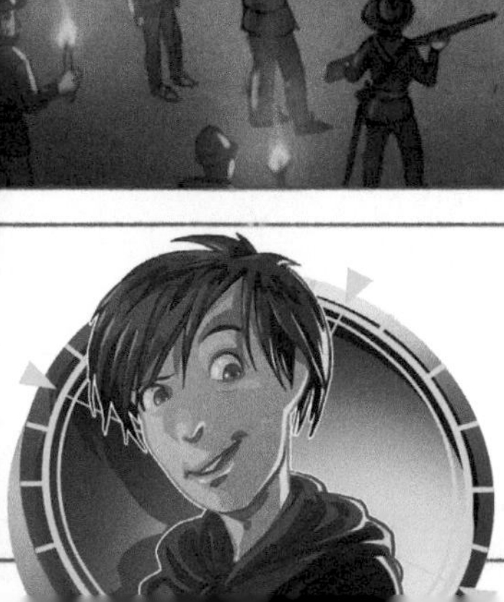

FLUX FACT

When the soldiers arrived at the farm, the Garrett family refused to tell them where Booth was hiding. John Garrett, a son of the farm's owner, revealed Booth's location only when Lieutenant Doherty threatened to shoot him.

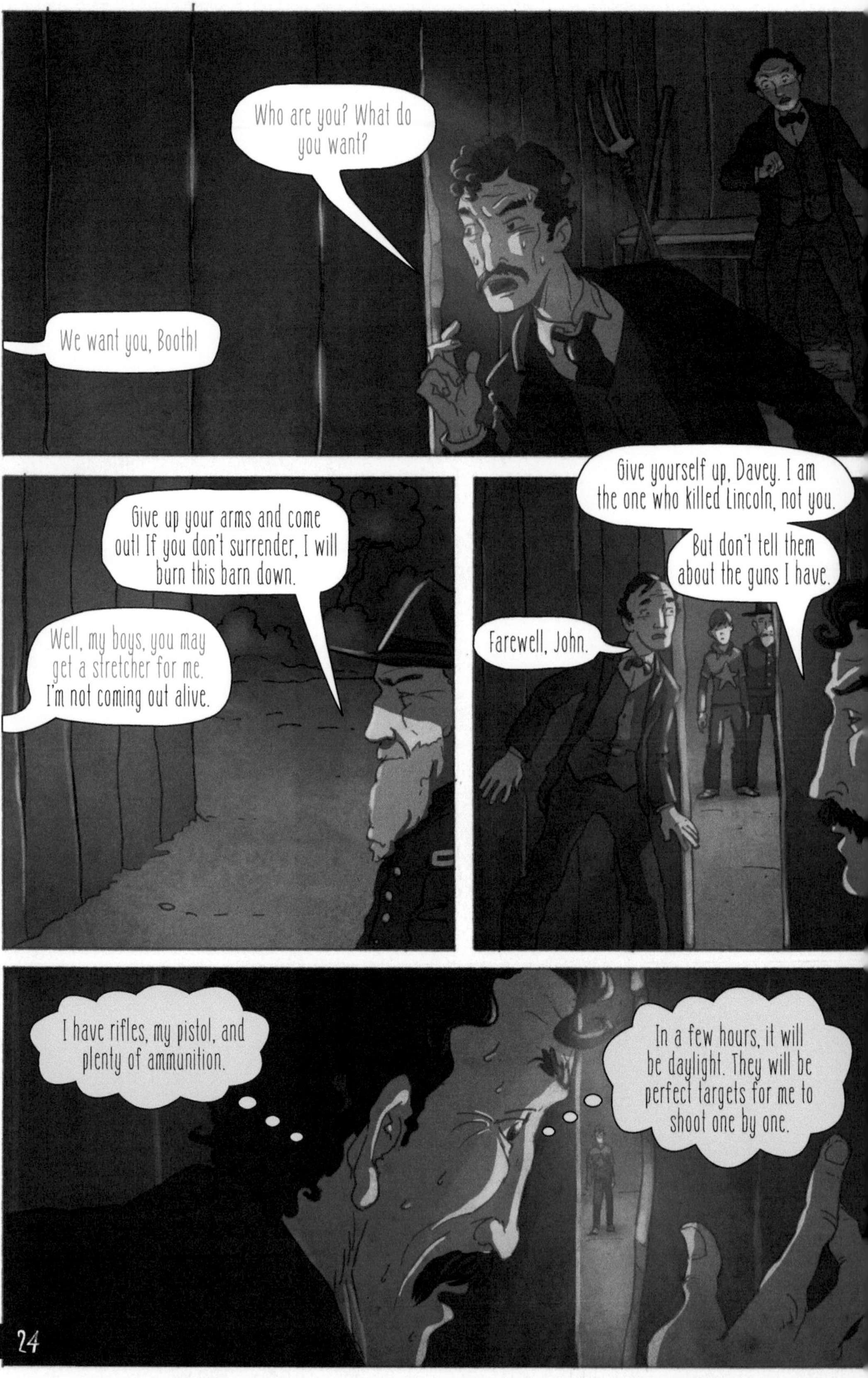

Who are you? What do you want?
We want you, Booth!
Give up your arms and come out! If you don't surrender, I will burn this barn down.
Well, my boys, you may get a stretcher for me. I'm not coming out alive.
Give yourself up, Davey. I am the one who killed Lincoln, not you.
But don't tell them about the guns I have.
Farewell, John.
I have rifles, my pistol, and plenty of ammunition.
In a few hours, it will be daylight. They will be perfect targets for me to shoot one by one.

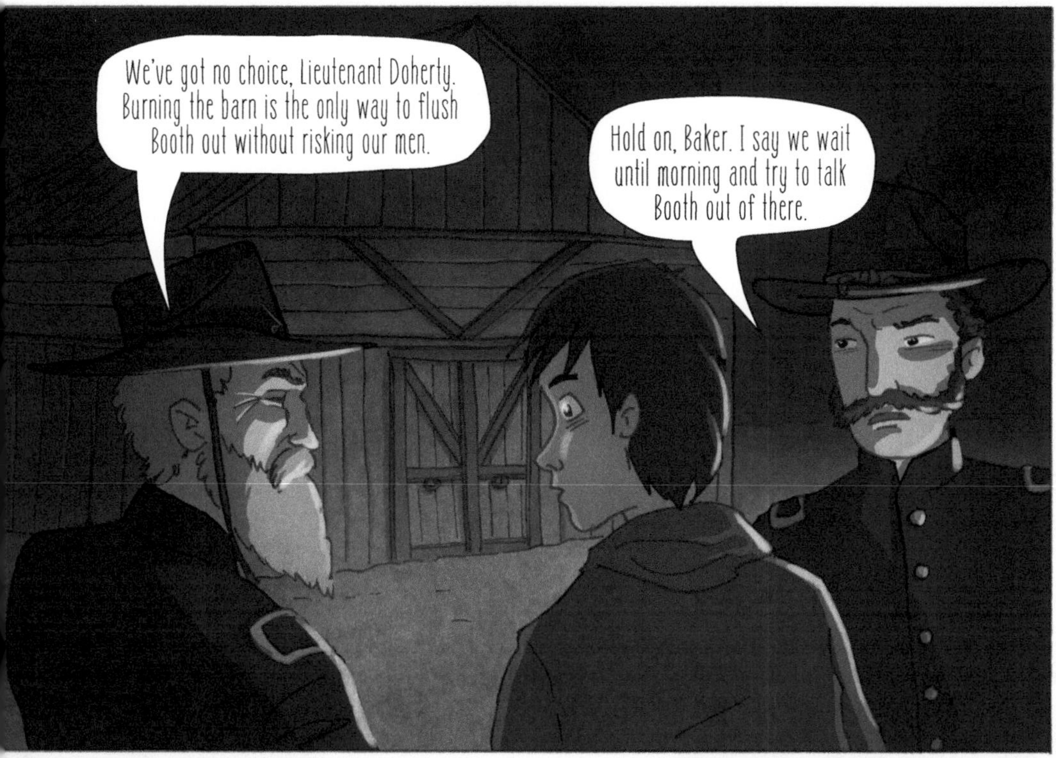
We've got no choice, Lieutenant Doherty. Burning the barn is the only way to flush Booth out without risking our men.
Hold on, Baker. I say we wait until morning and try to talk Booth out of there.

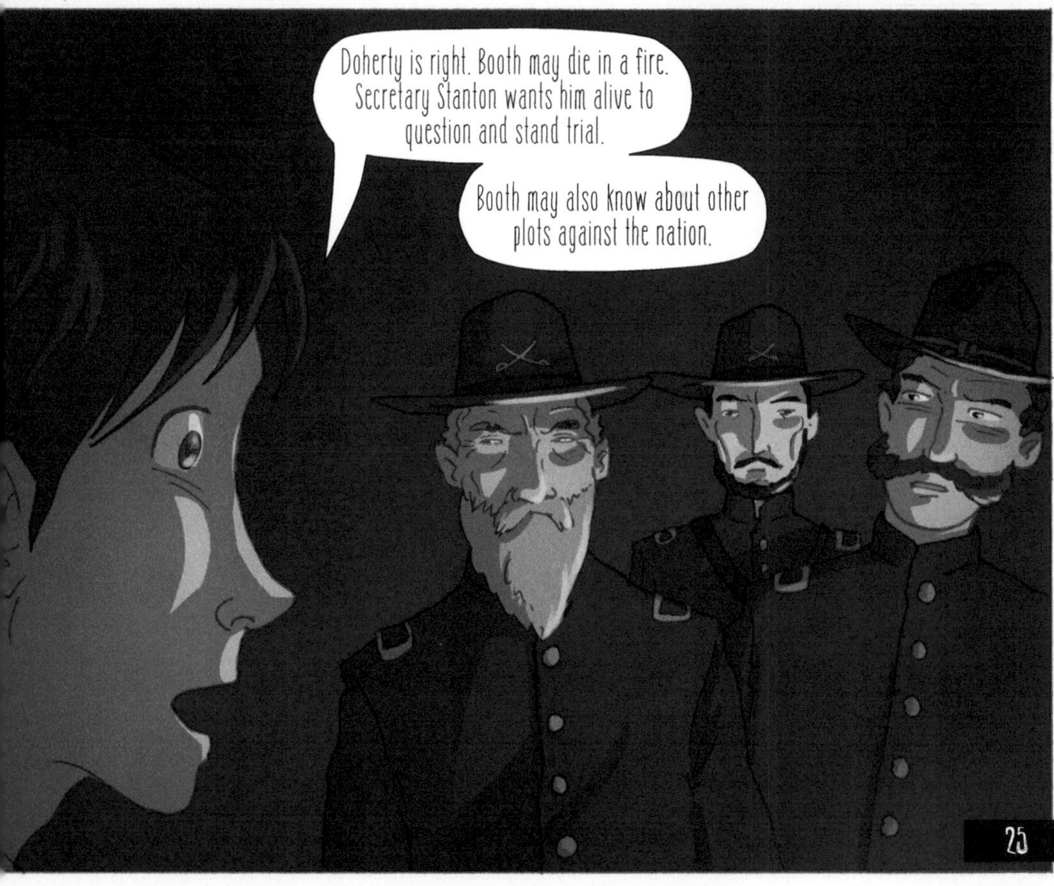
Doherty is right. Booth may die in a fire. Secretary Stanton wants him alive to question and stand trial.
Booth may also know about other plots against the nation.

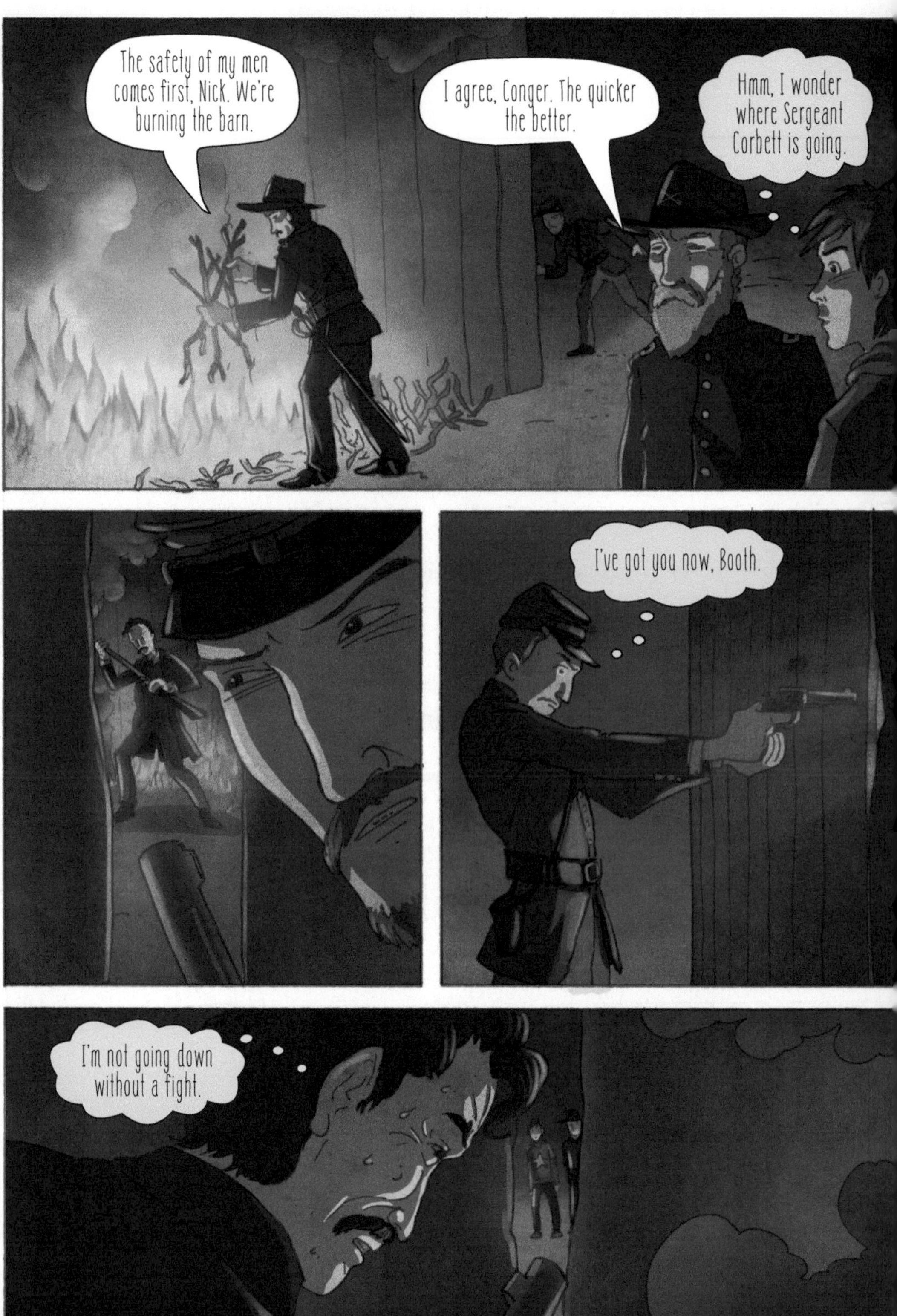
The safety of my men comes first, Nick. We're burning the barn.
I agree, Conger. The quicker the better.
Hmm, I wonder where Sergeant Corbett is going.
I've got you now, Booth.
I'm not going down without a fight.

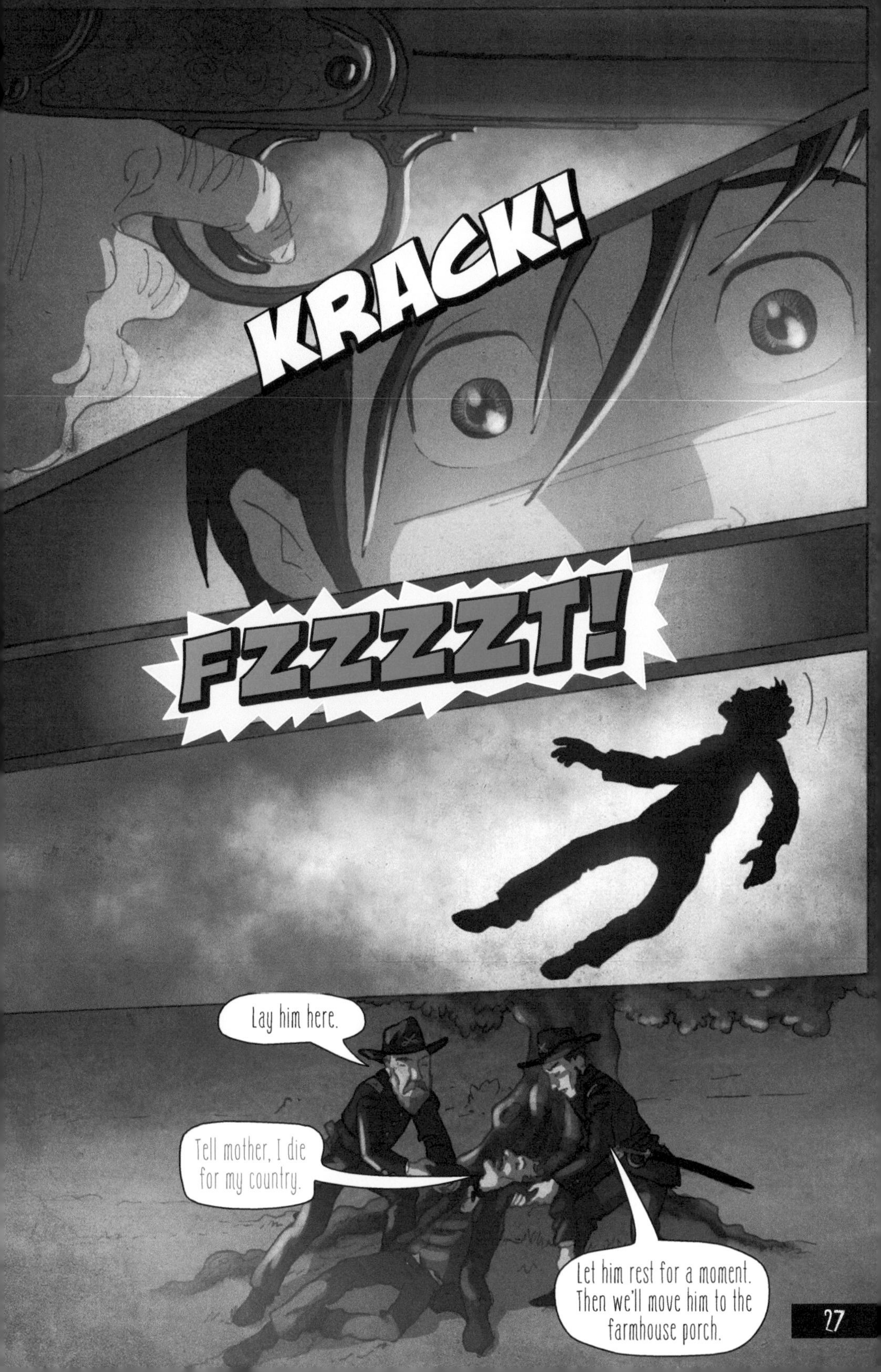
KRACK!
FZZZZT!
Lay him here.
Tell mother, I die for my country.
Let him rest for a moment. Then we'll move him to the farmhouse porch.

CHAPTER FIVE

AFTERMATH OF AN ASSASSINATION

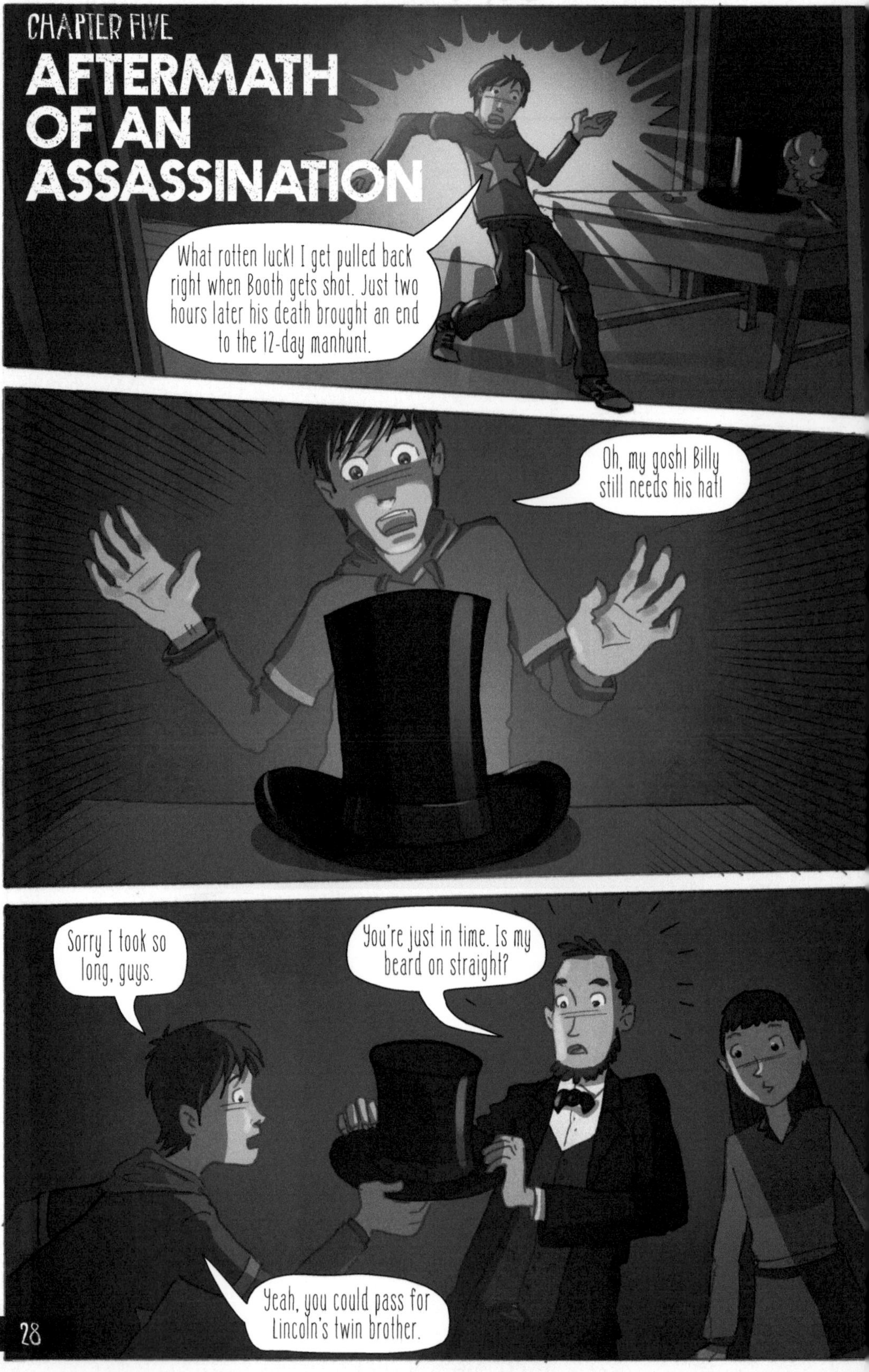
What rotten luck! I get pulled back right when Booth gets shot. Just two hours later his death brought an end to the 12-day manhunt.
Oh, my gosh! Billy still needs his hat!
Sorry I took so long, guys.
You're just in time. Is my beard on straight?
Yeah, you could pass for Lincoln's twin brother.

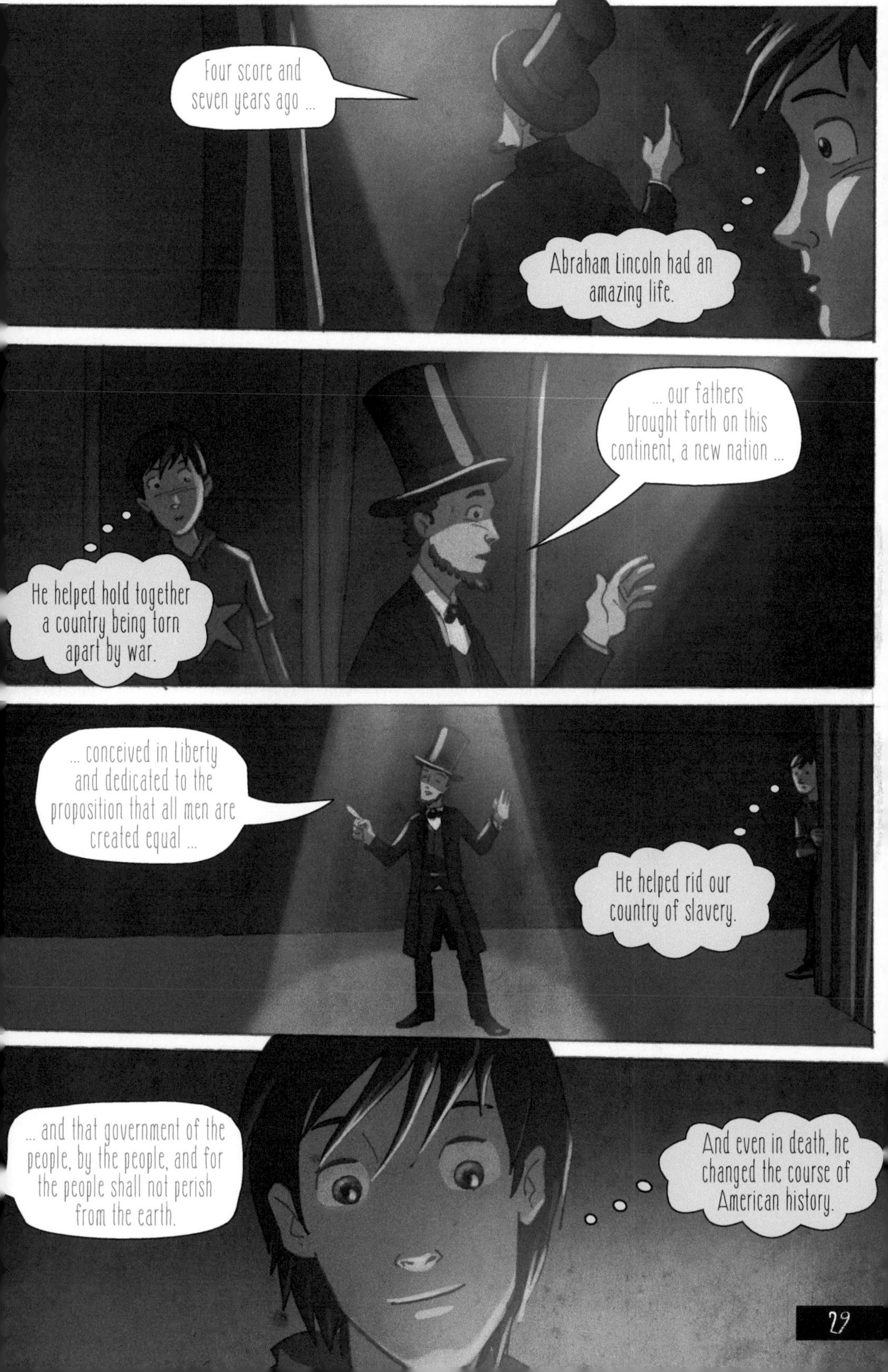
Four score and seven years ago ...
Abraham Lincoln had an amazing life.
... our fathers brought forth on this continent, a new nation ...
He helped hold together a country being torn apart by war.
... conceived in Liberty and dedicated to the proposition that all men are created equal ...
He helped rid our country of slavery.
... and that government of the people, by the people, and for the people shall not perish from the earth.
And even in death, he changed the course of American history.

FLUX FILES

MAJOR HENRY RATHBONE

Major Henry Rathbone struggled with Booth on the balcony of Ford's Theatre. He served in the Union Army during the Civil War (1861-1865) and was Lincoln's close friend. During the scuffle Booth slashed Rathbone's arm with his dagger.

END OF THE CIVIL WAR

The Confederacy surrendered to the Union on April 9, 1865, only five days before Booth assassinated Lincoln. The surrender marked the end of the Civil War, but there were still occasional fights between Confederate forces and Union troops, especially in the South. The hunt for Booth became more dangerous as U.S. troops moved farther south through Maryland and into Virginia.

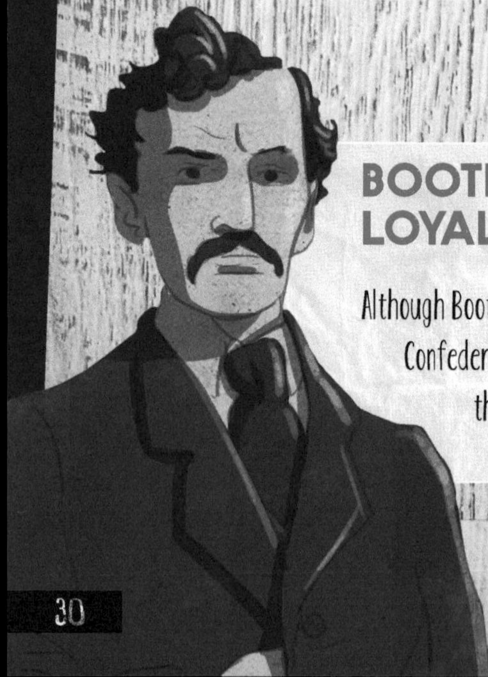

BOOTH'S CONFEDERATE LOYALTIES

Although Booth did not fight in the Civil War, he supported the Confederacy. He strongly opposed the abolition of slavery in the United States and hated Lincoln with a passion.

PLANNING THE ASSASSINATION

On the morning of April 14, Booth learned that Mr. and Mrs. Lincoln would be attending the play *Our American Cousin* at Ford's Theatre that night. He immediately made plans for the assassination. He told several accomplices of his plan and assigned them the job of killing Secretary of State William Seward and Vice President Andrew Johnson. He also planned his escape route out of Washington.

KIDNAPPING PLOT

Booth's original plan was to kidnap Lincoln. He hoped to exchange him for Confederate soldiers held in Union prison camps. Booth had learned Lincoln would be attending a play just outside Washington, D. C., on March 17, 1865. He and his accomplices plotted to overtake the president's carriage on the way there. But Lincoln changed his plans at the last minute and never went to the play. Booth abandoned his kidnapping plot.

BOOTH'S ACCOMPLICES

Many of Booth's suspected accomplices were captured and jailed. Eventually eight suspects were put on trial. All were found guilty on June 30, 1865. David Herold, Lewis Powell, George Atzerodt, and Mary Surratt were hanged. Atzerodt had planned to kill Vice President Johnson, but didn't carry out the attack. Mary Surratt had provided shelter for Booth and his accomplices. Samuel Arnold, Dr. Samuel Mudd, and Michael O'Laughlen received prison terms. Each were part of the kidnapping plot. Dr. Mudd also tended to Booth's broken leg. Edwin Spangler, who helped Booth escape from Ford's Theatre, also went to prison.

GLOSSARY

ABOLITION (ab-uh-LISH-uhn)—the immediate end of something, such as slavery

ACCOMPLICE (uh-KAHM-plis)—someone who helps another person commit a crime

ASSASSINATION (uh-sass-uh-NAY-shun)—the murder of someone who is well known or important

CONFEDERACY (kuhn-FE-druh-see)—the Southern states that fought against the Northern states in the Civil War; also called the Confederate States of America

CONSPIRATOR (kuhn-SPIR-uh-tor)—a plotter; someone who takes part in a conspiracy

REBEL (REB-uhl)—someone who fights against a government or the people in charge of something

TELEGRAPH (TEL-uh-graf)—a machine that uses electronic signals to send messages over long distances

TESTIMONY (TES-tuh-moh-nee)—evidence given by a witness in a trial

TYRANT (TYE-ruhnt)—someone who rules other people in a cruel or unjust way

UNION (YOON-yuhn)—the United States of America; also the Northern states that fought against the Southern states in the Civil War

VOLUNTEER (vol-uhn-TIHR)—people who offer to do a job, usually without pay

READ MORE

HALLY, ASHLEIGH. *Abraham Lincoln.* American Heroes. Hamilton, Ga.: State Standards Pub., 2012.

KEATING, FRANK. *Abraham.* A Paula Wiseman Book. New York: Simon & Schuster Books for Young Readers, 2015.

MARA, WIL. *Abraham Lincoln.* Rookie Biographies. New York: Children's Press, 2014.

SCHOTT, JANE A. *How Did Abraham Lincoln Make History?* Sterling History Maker Revisions. Minneapolis: Sandy Creek, 2014.

INTERNET SITES

FactHound offers a safe, fun way to find Internet sites related to this book. All sites on FactHound have been researched by our staff.

Here's all you do:

Visit *www.facthound.com*

Type in this code: 9781476502528

Super-cool stuff!

Check out projects, games and lots more at
www.capstonekids.com

INDEX

ABOUT THE AUTHOR

Nel Yomtov is a writer of children's nonfiction books and graphic novels. He specializes in writing about history, country studies, science, and biography. Nel has written frequently for Capstone, including other Nickolas Flux adventures such as *Defend Until Death!: Nickolas Flux and the Battle of the Alamo*; *Night of Rebellion!: Nickolas Flux and the Boston Tea Party*; and *Peril in Pompeii!: Nickolas Flux and the Eruption of Mount Vesuvius*. His graphic novel adaptation, *Jason and the Golden Fleece*, published by Stone Arch Books, was a winner of the 2009 Moonbeam Children's Book Award and the 2011 Lighthouse Literature Award. Nel lives in the New York City area.

ALL THE NICKOLAS FLUX ADVENTURES

ARRESTED FOR WITCHCRAFT!
NICKOLAS FLUX
AND THE SALEM WITCH TRIALS

DEFEND UNTIL DEATH!
NICKOLAS FLUX
AND THE BATTLE OF THE ALAMO

Flight to FREEDOM!
NICKOLAS FLUX
AND THE UNDERGROUND RAILROAD

Night of Rebellion!
NICKOLAS FLUX
AND THE BOSTON TEA PARTY

PERIL IN POMPEII!
NICKOLAS FLUX
AND THE ERUPTION OF MOUNT VESUVIUS

STAKE A CLAIM!
NICKOLAS FLUX
AND THE CALIFORNIA GOLD RUSH

READ THEM ALL!

SURPRISE ATTACK!
NICKOLAS FLUX
AND THE ATTACK ON PEARL HARBOR

TRACKING AN ASSASSIN!
NICKOLAS FLUX
AND THE ASSASSINATION OF ABRAHAM LINCOLN

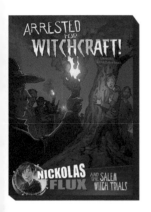

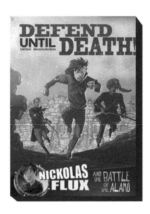

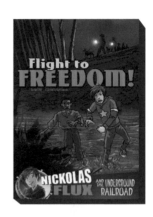

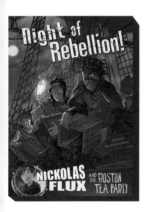

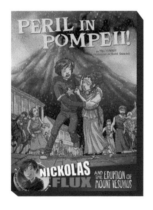

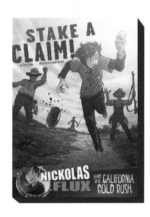

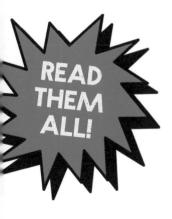

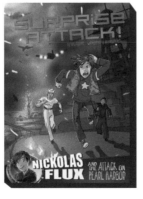

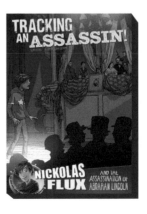